# ideals

# Gourmet on the Go
## COOKBOOK

by Naomi Arbit and June Turner

This cookbook has been created for the busy gourmet . . . the housewife and mother, the volunteer, the career girl, the bachelor . . . anyone who likes to eat well and to entertain, but who perhaps has neither the time nor the ability to spend unnecessary amounts of time or money. We have collected recipes which we think will meet these requirements.

It really is *easy* to be a good cook! It takes no more time or effort to cook well than it does to heat a frozen dinner or to fry a hamburger, and the rewards are instant and delicious. To cook creatively and economically is more difficult, but it *can* be done with a little ingenuity and a bit of planning. We all enjoy eating, and some of us must be the cooks . . . and we feel that it should be a pleasure to do both.

In these days of rising food prices, economical measures are a real necessity. Considering these facts, we have taken classic and traditional recipes and adapted them for modern cooks, making use of all the conveniences of the grocer's shelves and frozen foods and adding *the gourmet touch*.

Each recipe has been tested, tasted and approved by our families, friends and our cooking classes . . . stern critics whose tastes cover a broad range. They have been included because of their simplicity, clarity of directions, availability of ingredients and low cost of preparation.

We are sure you will enjoy these recipes, all done with *the gourmet touch*.

authors   *Naomi Arbit*
*June Turner*

*Sixth Printing*

ISBN 0-89542-631-5  295

# CONTENTS

## ABBREVIATIONS

t. — teaspoon
T — tablespoon
c. — cup
pkg. — package
pt. — pint
qt. — quart
oz. — ounce
lb. — pound

IDEALS PUBLISHING CORP., MILWAUKEE, WIS. 53201
© COPYRIGHT MCMLXXIV  PRINTED AND BOUND IN U.S.A.

## SHRIMP RÉMOULADE

"Shrimply" delicious and just a bit different. Tastes best if shrimp marinate overnight.

1½ lbs. hot, cooked shrimp
4 T. oil
2 T. olive oil
½ t. white pepper
½ t. salt
1 t. snipped parsley
½ t. horseradish
1 celery heart, minced
2 T. tarragon vinegar
4 T. brown mustard
½ c. green onions, snipped

Combine all ingredients. Whip with a fork or whisk until well blended and pour over hot shrimp. The shrimp must be hot to absorb the flavor of the marinade. Serve chilled in individual seafood shells or on a serving dish. Makes 8 to 10 servings.

## CAVIAR BALL

A spectacular addition to a cocktail buffet, or a jewel by itself for the cocktail hour.

1 8-oz. pkg. cream cheese
¼ t. bouillon crystals (dissolved in 1 t. hot water)
¼ t. minced onion
1 T. mayonnaise
2 4-oz. jars red or black caviar

Cream together cheese, bouillon and water, onion and mayonnaise. Shape into a ball. Frost completely with the caviar. Serve on a bed of endive or romaine lettuce, garnished with clusters of Olives à la Grecque (see accompaniments). Serve with rye saltines or melba toast.

## CHEESE BOREG

Keep a batch of unbaked Boreg in the freezer and be ready at an hour's notice to serve hors d'oeuvres hot from the oven.

    2 8-oz. pkgs. cream cheese, softened
 ½ lb. butter, softened
2¼ c. flour
 ¼ t. salt

Cream cheese and butter until well blended. To form dough, gradually add flour and salt until well blended. Divide into 4 equal balls and wrap each ball in waxed paper. Chill dough in refrigerator for at least 30 minutes. Roll out each ball of dough on a lightly floured piece of waxed paper to the thickness of pie-crust. Then cut out circles 2½ to 3 inches in diameter.

### FILLING

1½ lbs. mild brick cheese, grated
  1 egg, beaten
 ¼ c. chopped parsley (optional)

Combine cheese, egg and parsley. Place 1 teaspoon of filling on half of each circle, fold over, press edges shut on each side with fork tines. Bake on lightly greased cookie sheet in a preheated 350° oven 20 minutes, or until golden brown. Serve piping hot. Makes about 8 dozen.

Note: Allow frozen Boreg to thaw 30 minutes before baking.

---

Take a dip and dive in with raw vegetables. Try rutabaga, zucchini, cucumber or turnip slices cut with a crinkle cutter. Other favorites are raw mushrooms, cherry tomatoes, carrot sticks, celery, radishes, cauliflower buds.

---

## BOMBAY DIP

| | |
|---|---|
| 1 T. sugar | 1 t. grated onion |
| 1 t. garlic salt | 1 t. cider vinegar |
| 1 t. curry powder | ½ c. sour cream |
| 1 t. horseradish | ½ c. mayonnaise |

## GAUCHO DIP

  1 pkg. bleu cheese
  1 c. sour cream
  1 4-oz. can ripe olives, chopped
 ¼ t. garlic salt
  1 T. lemon juice

Combine all ingredients, chill and serve.

## CHOPPED LIVER (PÂTÉ)

Unlike French pâté, this calls for no marinating, no baking and no spirits. Children as well as adults will like its subtle flavor. Use as an hors d'oeuvre or as a first course.

  1 lb. calf's liver or chicken livers
  2 T. chicken fat or butter
  2 onions, sliced
  3 hard-cooked eggs
  4 T. chicken fat or butter, softened
  1 t. salt
 ¼ t. pepper
  1 T. mayonnaise

Gently sauté liver and onions in the 2 tablespoons of chicken fat or butter. When liver is no longer pink, remove liver and onions from pan and cool. Grind liver, onions and eggs together. Add the 4 tablespoons fat or butter, salt, pepper and mayonnaise and mix together thoroughly. Chill in bowl or mold. Turn out on a platter and serve with sliced cocktail rye bread or crackers. Or serve mounded on a lettuce leaf for individual first courses. Makes 12 to 14 servings.

Note: Create elegant Liver Pâté en Croûte by combining strudel dough (see cookie section) with a filling of this pâté. Completely enclose the filling and bake as directed. Slice and serve hot.

## CUCUMBER SANDWICHES

They look like ladies' tea sandwiches, but men like them.

  1 large cucumber, peeled
  1 8-oz. pkg. cream cheese, softened
 ½ t. garlic salt
 ½ t. Worcestershire sauce
  1 t. salt
 ¼ c. snipped green onion stems
     (or snipped chives)
     Rounds or fingers of sliced white bread
     Softened butter or margarine

Cut cucumber in half lengthwise. Run a teaspoon down the center, scraping to remove seeds. Dice, then drain in a strainer for at least 1 hour. Mix cream cheese, garlic salt, Worcestershire sauce and salt until well blended. Stir in drained cucumber and snipped onion stems. Spread on buttered bread rounds. Make open faced or closed. Refrigerate until serving time, covered with waxed paper and a damp cloth. Makes about 2½ dozen.

## QUICHE LORRAINE AU FROMAGE

This versatile dish with many variations can be a dinner-appetizer or a first course. It becomes an entrée served at a brunch, a luncheon or a midnight supper along with a tossed salad, fresh fruit and white wine.

1 9-inch pie shell*
1 c. grated Swiss cheese
4 eggs
1½ c. milk or light cream
¼ t. salt
⅛ t. pepper
⅛ t. nutmeg
2 T. butter, cut into dots

### OPTIONAL VARIATIONS

1 onion, sliced and sautéed
¼ lb. sliced, sautéed mushrooms
4 to 6 slices crisp, cooked bacon (or bacon substitute)
8 ozs. small cooked shrimp
7 ozs. crabmeat, flaked
1 pkg. drained, chopped spinach

Spread cheese and/or optional variations in pie shell. *(Use Foolproof Crust recipe in pie section, baking 7 minutes at 400°.) Lightly beat eggs and milk. Add salt, pepper and nutmeg and pour into pie shell. Distribute butter dots over top. Bake in a preheated 375° oven 35 to 40 minutes or until a knife inserted in center comes out clean. Allow to stand 10 minutes before cutting. Serves 4 to 6.

## CHEESE WAFERS

Your friends will think you are serving cookies with cocktails. A tasty surprise awaits them.

½ lb. sharp cheddar cheese, grated
¼ lb. butter or margarine, softened
½ t. salt
1½ c. sifted flour
Heavy pinch of cayenne pepper
Pecan halves or almond slivers (optional)

Cream together cheese, butter, salt and cayenne pepper. Add flour and mix into dough. Form into a roll, wrap in waxed paper and refrigerate. It will keep for a month. When needed, slice into thin wafers and bake on an ungreased cookie sheet in a preheated 350° oven 12 to 15 minutes. If desired, press a pecan half or almond sliver lightly into each wafer before baking. Makes 4 to 6 dozen wafers.

## SWISS ONION APPETIZERS

Swiss, swift and super! Prepare ahead and slide under the broiler just before serving.

Party rye, toasted rye chips or
bread rounds, toasted on one side
Mayonnaise
1 Bermuda onion
1 pkg. processed Swiss cheese

Spread untoasted side of bread with mayonnaise. Top with onion and cheese sliced to fit bread rounds. Place on a cookie sheet and broil until the cheese starts to melt. Serve while bubbly hot.

## NON-SWEDISH MEATBALLS

The secret ingredient is grape jelly. If you don't tell, no one will ever guess.

2 lbs. ground chuck, ground twice
1 grated onion
1 large raw potato, grated
1 egg
1 t. salt
1 clove garlic, minced
¼ t. pepper
1 bottle chili sauce
1 bottle water
1 small jar grape jelly

Mix meat, onion, potato, egg, salt, pepper and garlic together lightly. Shape into approximately 60 bite-sized balls. Bring chili sauce, water and jelly to a boil, reduce heat to a simmer and place the meatballs in the simmering sauce. Cover and cook 1 hour. Chill and remove layer of fat from top. Reheat and serve hot, in the sauce, in a chafing dish or freeze for future use.

## BRANDIED CHEESE

This spread may be prepared ahead, packed into crocks and chilled. It will keep refrigerated for as long as you can keep from eating it.

½ lb. bleu cheese, softened and crumbled
1 8-oz. pkg. cream cheese, softened
⅛ t. nutmeg
⅓ to ½ c. brandy

Cream together the softened cheeses with a pastry blender or fork. Stir in nutmeg and brandy, put into covered container and refrigerate. Bring to room temperature before serving.

# SOUPS AND STEWS

## CRAB BISQUE

At your next cocktail party make one for the road a steaming tureen of this delicious bisque. Your guests will thank you for it.

1 can tomato soup
1 can green pea soup
1 can consommé
2 soup cans milk
2 6-oz. pkgs. frozen Alaska crabmeat, thawed and drained
   Salt and pepper to taste
   Few drops of Worcestershire sauce
2 T. sherry

About 20 minutes before serving, mix together tomato soup, pea soup, consommé, milk, salt, pepper and Worcestershire sauce. Simmer for 10 minutes over low heat. Then add the crabmeat and simmer for 10 more minutes. Just before serving stir in the sherry. Makes 6 to 8 servings.

## QUICK ONION SOUP

The rich aroma and homemade taste of onion soup need not take hours. A few minutes to combine the ingredients, 30 minutes in the oven and voila!

3 large onions, sliced thin
3 cans consommé
1/8 lb. butter
1/4 c. red wine
1 c. grated Swiss or parmesan cheese
1 c. croutons

Melt butter and sauté onions until clear. Add consommé and wine. Pour into oven casserole, sprinkle with cheese and bake in a preheated 350° oven for 30 minutes. To brown the cheese, broil for a minute after cooking. Pass the croutons. Serves 4.

## COOL AS A CUCUMBER SOUP

An overture to an elegant dinner; serve in old-fashioned glasses.

1 c. sour cream
1 cucumber, peeled, seeded and sliced
1/4 t. dry mustard
1/2 t. instant chicken bouillon
1 T. snipped chives or 1 green onion
   Salt and pepper to taste

Put all ingredients into a blender and blend only until cucumber is finely chopped, not smooth. Chill and serve. Garnish with a sprinkle of dill or chives if desired. Makes 2 to 4 servings.

## ICED CHERRY SOUP

A lovely cooler!

2 c. sour pitted cherries
5½ c. water
1/2 c. sugar
1/2 lemon, thinly sliced
1 stick cinnamon
3 T. cornstarch
1/2 t. salt
1/2 t. almond extract
1/2 t. red food coloring
1 c. sour cream

Mash cherries slightly in soup pot. Add 5 cups water with sugar, lemon slices and cinnamon. Cover and cook slowly for 30 minutes. Dissolve cornstarch in remaining 1/2 cup water and add to cherry mixture with salt, extract and coloring. Cook until soup clears and begins to thicken. Serve cold with a generous dollop of sour cream on each portion. Makes 4 to 6 servings.

## NEW ENGLAND CLAM CHOWDER

You don't have to dig clams to dig this chowder — everything is out of a can!

1 can cream of celery soup
2 cans cream of potato soup
2 cans minced or chopped clams
2 soup cans milk
3 slices bacon, fried and crumbled (optional)
1/2 small onion, minced
   Dash of marjoram

Mix all the ingredients together, heat until piping hot and serve. Makes 4 to 6 servings.

# WINTER GAZPACHO

We call this recipe Winter Gazpacho because it has canned tomatoes. It's a touch of summer to brighten the dreary winter.

2 large cans whole tomatoes
1 cucumber, peeled and finely chopped
1 green pepper, finely chopped
1 small onion, finely chopped
6 stalks celery, finely chopped
6 sweet pickle slices, finely chopped
3 T. pimiento, chopped
3 T. capers
2 T. wine vinegar
¼ t. dry mustard
3 T. salad oil
3 T. olive oil
½ t. salt
¼ t. pepper, freshly ground
  Few drops of tabasco

Drain tomatoes, save juice. Place tomatoes, oils, mustard, vinegar, salt, pepper and tabasco in blender and blend at low speed for about 1 minute. Tomatoes should be in small pieces. Pour into the tomato juice and stir in cucumber, green pepper, onion, celery, pickle, pimiento and capers. Chill until very cold. Makes 4 to 8 servings.

## VEGETABLE SOUP

The aroma of vegetable soup on a winter's day brings a feeling of warmth and hungry anticipation. It must simmer for several hours and really tastes best on the second day.

 1 lb. chuck
 1 or 2 pieces of short rib (or a soupbone)
 2 large cans tomatoes
 3 cans water (or enough to cover vegetables)
 1 or 2 small turnips, peeled and diced
 ¼ head cabbage, shredded
 2 medium onions, chopped
 2 t. salt
 ½ t. pepper
 2 t. thyme
 1 bay leaf (optional)
 ¼ to ½ c. Burgundy wine
 3 to 4 c. assorted fresh vegetables
    (or 2 pkgs. frozen mixed vegetables)

Brown meat, add vegetables, liquids and seasonings, simmer slowly for 3 to 5 hours. After soup has chilled, fat may be easily removed.

## SAILOR'S STEW

Piping hot sailor's stew tastes delicious on a cold day.

 ½ lb. bacon, cut up
 2 onions, chopped
 1 can corn
 1 can peas
 1 can kidney beans
 1 can tomatoes
    Salt and pepper to taste

Sauté bacon and onions and pour off fat. Add remaining ingredients and simmer until thick. Makes 4 to 6 servings.

## QUICK SENEGALESE SOUP

Chicken curry soup: Cold for a hot day, hot for a cold day.

 2 10½-oz. cans cream of chicken soup
 1 soup can light cream
 2 t. curry powder
 4 to 6 thin lemon slices

Combine soup, cream and curry powder and mix until smooth; use a blender if desired. Serve hot or cold garnished with lemon slices. Makes 4 to 6 servings.

## COLD SPINACH SOUP

Keep your cool in the summer.

 1 pkg. frozen chopped spinach
 2 T. instant chicken bouillon
 ¼ pt. half-and-half sour cream
 3 c. water
    Salt to taste

Partially thaw spinach; break into small chunks. Put into a blender with half of the water and blend. Add remaining water and seasonings and mix again. Add sour cream and blend. Chill thoroughly and serve garnished with chopped hard-cooked egg or diced cucumber. Serves 4.

## FRENCH PUMPKIN SOUP

If you can't bear to throw away the jack-o'-lantern, the French have a delightful solution.

 1 fresh pumpkin, peeled
    (or 6 c. canned pumpkin, without spices)
 3 c. heavy cream
 ½ t. salt
 ¼ t. white pepper

Cut the pumpkin into pieces, remove seeds and stringy parts. Drop into boiling salted water and cook until tender, about 30 minutes. Drain and put through a food mill. Season to taste with salt and pepper. Add cream, blend well, heat and serve.

If using canned pumpkin, blend pumpkin, salt, pepper and cream. Heat and serve. Makes 4 to 6 servings.

## LEMON SOUP

This is a proper start for a Greek dinner.

 6 c. chicken broth
 ⅓ c. raw rice
 2 egg yolks
    Juice of 1 lemon

Bring chicken broth to a boil and add rice. Simmer for 30 minutes or until rice is tender. Beat egg yolks and lemon juice until frothy, and slowly stir into 1 cup of the broth. Pour this mixture back into the rest of the soup, stirring constantly. Reheat to just below the boiling point and serve immediately. Serves 6.

## CRANBERRY SHRUB

A twist of the wrist and you have a refreshing start for brunch, luncheon or dinner.

1 pt. chilled cranberry juice
1 6-oz. can frozen pineapple juice
5 7-oz. bottles carbonated lemon-lime
  beverage
1 pt. lemon ice

Combine juices. Slowly add the chilled lemon-lime beverage. Float a spoonful of lemon ice in each glass.

## SPICED CRANBERRIES

A tart and refreshing new way to serve fresh cranberries. This is a crisp and spicy accompaniment for meat or poultry.

1 lb. fresh cranberries
2 c. sugar
1 c. water
5 whole cloves
2 whole allspice
2 3-inch cinnamon sticks

Wash berries, remove stems, drain. In a large saucepan, combine sugar and water and bring to a boil over medium heat. Stir constantly until sugar dissolves. Add cloves, allspice, cinnamon; reduce heat and simmer 5 minutes. Add cranberries and stir one or two times until berries start to pop, about 3 minutes. Remove from heat and cool. Pour into a 1-quart jar and refrigerate, covered, for several days before serving. Keeps indefinitely.

## OLIVES À LA GRECQUE

Ripe olives in this spicy marinade will keep for months in your refrigerator, ready for last-minute snacking. They also add a Greek touch to a plain tossed salad.

2 large cans pitted black olives
½ c. vinegar
1 c. olive oil
1 bay leaf
1 clove garlic, cut in half
1 t. oregano

Drain liquid from olives. Mix vinegar, oil, bay leaf, garlic and oregano together and pour over olives. Refrigerate in a covered jar. Bring to room temperature at least 1 hour before serving. Remove olives from marinade, drain and serve.

# ACCOMPANIMENTS

## CARRIE NASH'S CHUTNEY

Serve this irresistible chutney with chicken, turkey, duck, beef, lamb or pork as well as curried dishes. The recipe makes over a quart, so take some to a friend. A gift from your kitchen is truly one of a kind.

2 c. sugar
1¼ c. white vinegar
¼ c. Sauterne or apple wine (optional)
2 oranges, diced with rind
1 lemon, diced with rind
1 lime, diced with rind
1 medium onion, diced
1 clove garlic, minced
1 c. white raisins
2¾ ozs. crystallized ginger, diced
2½ lbs. peaches, peeled and diced
  (or 2½ lbs. pears, unpeeled and diced)

Bring sugar, vinegar and wine to a boil and cook for 10 to 15 minutes. Add remaining ingredients and simmer for 30 minutes. Makes over 1 quart.

## SPEEDY PICKLES

Pickled cucumbers are Scandinavian favorites.

2 cucumbers
1 c. white vinegar
½ c. water
½ c. sugar
1 t. salt
2 t. mixed pickling spices
  (tied in a cloth bag)

Slice 2 unpeeled cucumbers paper-thin and place in cold water for 1 hour. Drain well. Combine all ingredients in a saucepan and boil until the pickles are transparent. Remove spice bag and chill in liquid before serving.

# BEEF AND PEPPERS

Inexperienced western chefs will become masters of Oriental cookery with Beef and Peppers, which is eating at its best.

1½ lbs. beef (tenderloin, sirloin or flank steak)
1 clove garlic, minced
½ t. ginger
1 T. soy sauce
1 t. oil
2 t. cornstarch
Oil
2 sliced Bermuda or sweet onions
2 green peppers, quartered
2 tomatoes, quartered
1 t. sugar
1 c. canned bouillon (or consommé)
1 T. cornstarch
1 t. soy sauce
¼ c. cold water
2 T. sherry

Cut meat diagonally into thin strips while partially frozen. Combine garlic, ginger, 1 tablespoon soy sauce, 1 teaspoon oil and 2 teaspoons cornstarch. Add beef, toss lightly. Sauté small amounts of meat in hot oil quickly until done. Remove meat and keep warm.

Add oil to pan, heat, sauté onions and green peppers for about 2 to 3 minutes. Add stock, bring to a boil. Blend 1 tablespoon cornstarch and the water together. Add to hot mixture with 1 teaspoon soy sauce and the sugar. Cook, stirring constantly, about 2 minutes. Add meat, sherry and tomatoes to sauce. Warm thoroughly and serve with rice. Makes 4 servings.

## BEEF BURGUNDY

Classically French in origin, but simplified in our presentation, this dish gains in flavor as it cooks. It may be prepared in advance, then refrigerated or frozen.

2 lbs. lean stew beef, cut into cubes
2 T. flour
2 T. butter
1 T. olive oil
1 t. salt
¼ t. pepper
2 c. beef consommé
1 c. Burgundy wine
1 medium onion, chopped
1 carrot, sliced
1 clove garlic, minced
1 bay leaf
¼ t. thyme
1 jar small whole onions
   (or ½ pkg. frozen)
1 can sliced mushrooms
1 T. snipped parsley

Toss the meat in flour, salt and pepper and brown in fat. Add consommé, wine, onion, carrot, garlic, bay leaf and thyme. Simmer 2½ to 3 hours until meat is tender. Add parsley, onions and mushrooms just before serving and simmer until hot.

If more liquid is needed during cooking, add consommé and wine in proportions of 2 parts consommé to 1 part wine. Makes 4 to 6 servings.

## ROAST BEEF TENDERLOIN

For that special dinner, be extravagant and roast a whole beef tenderloin.

1 4- to 4½-lb. beef tenderloin
½ c. oil
½ c. Burgundy wine
2 T. grated onion
1 clove garlic, minced
1½ t. salt
5 drops tabasco (optional)

Combine all ingredients and allow beef to marinate in refrigerator at least 2 hours. Remove from sauce. Preheat oven to 450°. Place meat in a shallow pan and brush with marinade. Bake for 15 minutes. Reduce temperature to 350°. Baste with marinade occasionally and continue baking for 35 minutes for medium rare, or less time for rare. Serve garnished with sautéed mushroom caps and sprigs of parsley. Makes 6 servings.

## LONDON BROIL

For years well-known restaurants have used flank steaks to create a gourmet treat. The secret lies in the marinade and in the cooking and cutting techniques. Try both of these: one with an Oriental touch, the other with a French flair. They are deliciously different, each with its own distinctive flavor.

### ORIENTAL

1 or 2 flank steaks
2 cloves garlic, minced
¼ c. crystallized ginger, chopped
¼ c. lemon juice
¼ c. soy sauce
¼ t. pepper

### FRENCH

1 or 2 flank steaks
½ c. oil
½ c. Burgundy wine
2 T. minced onion
1 clove garlic, minced
1½ t. salt
5 drops tabasco

Score both sides of the steaks in a diamond pattern about ⅛-inch deep. Combine all ingredients in a large, shallow baking dish. Coat steaks with the marinade and turn four times during a 2-hour period of marinating in the refrigerator. Remove steak from the marinade and broil for 7 minutes on each side. To serve, cut steak diagonally into thin slices. Makes 4 to 6 servings.

## ONE-RIB BEEF ROAST

Small families can enjoy prime rib of beef.

One-rib roast, 3 to 4 lbs.
2 T. butter
1 clove garlic, minced
Salt and pepper to taste

Mix minced garlic with softened butter and spread on both sides of the roast. Place roast on rack in shallow pan. Broil 3½ to 4 inches from heat until brown. Turn and brown other side. Sprinkle with salt and pepper and roast in a 350° oven about 9 minutes per pound for a medium-well-done roast. Makes 4 servings.

## BRISKET OF BEEF

Prepare this brisket the day before you serve it and be a relaxed hostess as it heats in the oven. It holds beautifully for hours and can be covered lightly with foil if it starts to dry out.

    1  5-lb. brisket of beef
    2  t. salt
    ¼  t. pepper
    2  onions, sliced
    4  stalks celery
    1  c. catsup
    8  ozs. beer

Place beef in roaster, fat side up. Season with salt and pepper. Place onions, celery and catsup over the beef. Put ¼ cup water in bottom of pan. Roast in a preheated 350° oven uncovered, basting until well browned. Cover. After about 3 hours, pour the beer over the beef, recover and cook until tender. Remove meat from gravy. Strain gravy and chill until fat rises and solidifies. Remove layer of fat.

Slice chilled meat and reheat in gravy. Add ½ cup water if necessary. If a thicker gravy is desired, place cooked onions and celery in a blender with the skimmed gravy and blend until smooth. Serves 8.

## TEN-MINUTE SUKIYAKI

Be a minute miser. Using your electric frying pan, cook and serve at the table, Japanese-style.

    3  T. oil
    1  medium sliced onion
    4  large sliced mushrooms
    ½  lb. thinly sliced beef
    ¼  lb. fresh spinach
    3  5-inch pieces celery,
       thinly sliced
    4  T. soy sauce
    2  T. sugar
    ½  can consommé
    4  scallions

Sauté onion in oil, add mushrooms and meat, cook 2 minutes. Add spinach and cook 1 minute; add celery and cook 1 minute. Cut scallions lengthwise into thin pieces. Add to mixture. Then add soy sauce, cook 1 minute. Add sugar and consommé and cook 2 minutes. Use thinly sliced rare roast beef if desired (10 minutes). Makes 2 to 3 servings. Repeat as often as necessary.

## SPEEDY SAUERBRATEN

Be a kitchen wizard and use your leftover roast beef to make this taste-tempting German entrée.

    2  T. butter
    1  small onion, chopped
    ¼  c. celery, chopped
    ½  c. dark raisins
    2  T. catsup
    1  T. cider vinegar
    ¼  c. crumbled gingersnaps
    ¼  t. dry mustard
    ½  c. water
    1  can bouillon
    1  T. cornstarch
       Sliced roast beef

Sauté onion and celery in butter for 5 minutes. Add raisins, vinegar, catsup and gingersnaps mixed with dry mustard. Add water and stir. Dissolve cornstarch in 2 tablespoons of the bouillon. Add with remaining bouillon and cook, stirring constantly, until clear. Add sliced beef to the sauce, cover and simmer for 15 minutes. Serve on a bed of noodles. Sprinkle with poppy seeds if desired. Makes 2 to 4 servings.

## GLAZED CORNED BEEF, HAM OR CANADIAN BACON

Glistening with a pineapple glaze, corned beef never dressed like this before.

    1  corned beef, ham or Canadian bacon,
       cooked
    8  to 10 whole cloves
    2  t. mustard
    ½  c. brown sugar
    ½  c. bread crumbs
    1  medium can crushed pineapple, drained

Place meat in foil-lined roasting pan. Score top and stud with whole cloves. Mix mustard, brown sugar, bread crumbs and pineapple together and coat top of the meat. Bake in a preheated 325° oven 45 to 60 minutes until heated through. Watch for scorching. Add a little water if necessary.

---

It is easier to slice meat, fish or fowl if they are partially frozen.

## STEAK DIANE

Make like a maitre'd — prepare and flame this dish at your dinner table.

    4  tenderloin or rib-eye steaks,
       (¼- to ½-inch thick)
    4  T. butter
    4  T. snipped chives
    4  T. snipped parsley
    1  t. Dijon mustard
    1  t. Worcestershire sauce
    ¼  t. salt
    ¼  t. pepper
    ½  c. dry vermouth
    ¼  c. brandy

In a large chafing dish or electric frying pan, melt 2 tablespoons of the butter and brown steaks quickly, turning once. Remove to platter. Add remaining butter, chives, parsley, mustard, Worcestershire sauce, salt and pepper and bring to a light boil. Add vermouth and simmer, stirring occasionally for 2 to 3 minutes. Heat brandy in a small saucepan (do not boil). Return steaks to skillet. Pour heated brandy over steaks and flame. Serve as soon as flame dies, spooning sauce over the steaks.

## BEEF STROGANOFF

Traditional Russian Stroganoff, with a little wine for additional zest, is easy, quick and delicious.

    2 to 2½ lbs. beef (tenderloin, sirloin or
       flank steak)
    3  T. flour
    ½  t. salt
    ¼  t. pepper
    3  T. fat
    3  onions, sliced thin
    ½  c. tomato juice
    1  can consommé
    ½  t. sugar
    ½  c. sour cream
    ½  lb. sliced mushrooms
    3  T. Burgundy wine (optional)

Cut meat in thin strips. Toss in flour, salt and pepper. Brown meat and onions in 3 tablespoons hot fat. Add tomato juice, consommé and sugar. Reduce heat and simmer until meat is tender. Blend in sour cream, mushrooms and wine. Heat but do not boil. Serve over buttered noodles, rice or mashed potatoes. Makes 4 to 6 servings.

## STUFFED STEAK

Try this succulent and mouth-watering way to dress up a steak.

    1  3-lb. sirloin steak, cut 1¼-inch thick
    2  T. butter or margarine
    1  8-oz. can mushrooms, drained
    2  green onions, chopped
    1  T. flour
    2  T. parsley, snipped
    1  T. lemon juice
    1  T. Worcestershire sauce
       Salt and pepper to taste

Cut a pocket in the steak with a sharp knife. The pocket should be the length of the steak and almost all the way from side to side.

Melt butter and sauté onions and mushrooms until onions are soft. Stir in flour, then add lemon juice and Worcestershire sauce and stir until thickened. Add parsley.

Fill the pocket in the steak with the stuffing. Put three or four toothpicks along the edge to keep the pocket closed.

Broil for 10 to 12 minutes on each side. Salt and pepper to taste. Makes 6 to 8 servings.

## BEEF BISTRO

A Spanish dish, full flavored but not spicy hot.

    1½ lbs. boneless top round
    1  green pepper, chopped
    1  onion, chopped
    2  ribs of celery, sliced
    1  clove garlic, minced
    1  can sliced mushrooms
       (or ½ lb. fresh mushrooms)
    1  can tomato soup
    1  jar stuffed olives, drained and sliced
    ½  c. Burgundy wine

Trim meat, then cut in strips or cubes and brown in fat. Add green pepper, onion, celery, garlic, mushrooms and soup and simmer, covered, for 45 to 60 minutes. Add wine and olives 10 to 15 minutes before serving. Add ⅓ cup water if there is insufficient sauce. Yield: 4 servings.

## SPAGHETTI SAUCE

Spaghetti sauce need not simmer all day long. This one will be ready before you have finished setting the table and cooking the pasta.

  1 lb. ground chuck (optional)
  3 T. olive oil
  1 medium onion, chopped
  2 cloves garlic, minced
  1 1-lb. can tomatoes
  1 6-oz. can tomato paste
¼ t. oregano
⅛ t. thyme
⅛ t. basil
½ c. sweet vermouth

Brown meat, drain fat. Sauté onions and garlic in olive oil until golden. Add meat and remaining ingredients. Simmer until smooth and thick, about 35 minutes. Serve over cooked spaghetti (makes enough for 1 pound). Sprinkle with grated parmesan cheese. Serves 4.

Cook the pasta (spaghetti) until al dente (slightly chewy) — about 8 to 10 minutes in rapidly boiling water (check package for directions).

## LASAGNE

  1 lb. ground round or chuck
  1 clove garlic, minced
  1 T. parsley flakes
  1 T. basil
1½ t. salt
  1 1-lb. can tomatoes
  2 6-oz. cans tomato paste

Brown meat, drain fat. Add next 6 ingredients. Simmer about 30 minutes, stirring occasionally.

  1 pkg. lasagne noodles, cooked
     and rinsed in cold water
  3 c. small curd, creamed cottage cheese
  2 eggs, slightly beaten
  2 T. parsley flakes
  2 t. salt
½ t. pepper
½ c. grated parmesan cheese
  1 lb. mozzarella cheese, sliced thin

Combine cottage cheese, eggs, parsley flakes, salt, pepper and parmesan cheese. Place half of the cooked noodles in a 13 x 9-inch baking dish. Spread half of the cheese mixture, half of the mozzarella, half of the meat sauce over the noodles. Repeat layers, ending with meat sauce. Decorate top with triangles of mozzarella. Bake in a preheated 375° oven for 30 minutes. Let stand 10 to 15 minutes before serving. Cut into squares if desired. Makes 8 to 10 servings.

## POLYNESIAN SWEET-SOUR MEATBALLS

Enjoy meatballs with the flavor of the Islands.

- 1 lb. ground round
- 1 egg
- 2 T. flour
- ½ t. salt
  Dash of pepper
- 3 T. oil
- 1 c. chicken bouillon
- 2 large green peppers, cut in small pieces
- 4 slices canned pineapple, cut in pieces
- 3 T. cornstarch
- ½ c. sugar
- 1 T. soy sauce
- ½ c. vinegar
- ½ c. pineapple juice

Shape meat into 16 balls. Combine egg, flour, salt and pepper to make a smooth batter. Heat oil in a large skillet. Dip meatballs in batter and fry until brown on all sides. Remove from pan and keep warm. Pour out all but 1 tablespoon of fat. Add ½ cup of the bouillon, the green peppers and the pineapple. Cover and cook over medium heat for 5 minutes.

Blend cornstarch, sugar, soy sauce, vinegar, pineapple juice and remaining bouillon. Add to skillet and cook, stirring constantly, until mixture comes to a boil and thickens. Return meatballs to sauce and heat. Serve with rice. Yield: 4 servings.

## MEAT BLINTZES

A hostess with flair will appreciate a dish hearty enough to stand alone on the menu.

- 1 lb. ground beef (sautéed and drained) or cooked chicken or leftover roast, ground
- 1 egg
- 1 T. instant minced onion
- 1 t. salt
- ¼ t. pepper

Make blintzes (see bread section). Mix above ingredients together. Place 1 heaping teaspoonful on each blintz and fold envelope-style. Brown blintzes as directed in recipe and serve with applesauce or sour cream. Makes 22 to 24 blintzes.

Note: These blintzes may be frozen and thawed in refrigerator before browning.

## MOUSSAKA

Traditionally, Moussaka is made with ground lamb. Ground beef may be substituted for lamb, or use half beef and half lamb.

- 1 eggplant, peeled and sliced
- 1 lb. ground chuck
- 1 medium onion, chopped
- 1 clove garlic, minced
- 1 1-lb. can tomatoes
- ½ t. oregano
- 1 t. salt
- ⅛ t. pepper
- 1 T. olive oil
- ½ c. cottage cheese
- 2 eggs, slightly beaten
  Nutmeg

Sauté meat, onion and garlic until meat is brown. Drain well. Add tomatoes, oregano, salt, pepper. Simmer 10 minutes.

Brush eggplant slices with olive oil and broil for 5 minutes on each side. Make layers of eggplant and meat sauce in a greased casserole. Top with cottage cheese and eggs beaten together. Sprinkle with a little nutmeg. Bake in a preheated 350° oven for 2 hours. Serves 4.

## STUFFED PEPPERS

A natural for summer menus when peppers are plentiful.

- 6 green peppers
- 3 T. chopped onion
- 2 T. butter
- 1 lb. ground chuck
- ½ c. cooked rice
- ½ t. salt
- ¼ t. pepper
- 2 8-oz. cans tomato sauce
- ¼ c. sherry
- ½ c. sour cream
- ¼ lb. sharp cheddar cheese, grated or shredded

Remove stem ends and seeds from peppers. Sauté onion in butter, add meat and brown. Mix in rice, salt and pepper and 1 can tomato sauce. Fill peppers and arrange in a baking dish. Combine sour cream, the remaining can of tomato sauce and the sherry and pour over peppers. Bake in a preheated 350° oven 45 to 60 minutes. Sprinkle with the cheese and bake another 15 minutes. Makes 4 to 6 servings.

## MEAT LOAF WELLINGTON

An old friend takes on a new look. Dress your meat loaf in style with a flaky brown crust.

2 eggs
1 can cream of mushroom soup
1 c. dry bread crumbs
1 T. mustard
3 lb. lean ground beef
2 T. instant minced onion
2 t. salt
2 t. Worcestershire sauce
2 T. catsup
1 can crescent roll dough

Combine all ingredients except dough and press mixture into a loaf pan. Bake in a preheated 350° oven for 1½ hours. Cool in pan for 5 minutes. Drain off fat and invert meat loaf onto a cookie sheet.

Separate roll dough into 4 rectangles. Overlap slightly on a pastry cloth or floured board to form a large rectangle. Roll out to form a 10 x 15-inch rectangle. Drape over meat loaf, covering all visible sides. Trim excess dough; it can be used to make a braided design on top. Brush top and sides with slightly beaten egg white. Bake in a preheated 325° oven for 15 to 20 minutes or until golden brown. Yield: 6 to 8 servings.

## HAMBURGER STROGANOFF

Dinner on the double.

1 lb. ground chuck
½ lb. mushrooms, sliced (or 1 can, drained)
2 small onions, chopped
3 T. butter
2 T. flour
1 can beef consommé
1 T. tomato paste or catsup
1 t. Worcestershire sauce
½ t. salt
⅛ t. pepper
1 c. sour cream
   Paprika

Sauté meat, onions and mushrooms in butter. Drain excess fat. Sprinkle with flour, stir lightly, add consommé and stir until smooth and slightly thickened. Add tomato paste, Worcestershire sauce, salt and pepper. Simmer and stir for 10 minutes. Just before serving stir in sour cream (do not boil). Sprinkle with paprika. Serve over noodles, rice or toasted English muffins. Serves 4.

## FILLED CABBAGE

Double the recipe while you have the kettle on. It improves with age (make a day ahead). It can also be frozen.

1 cabbage
1 lb. ground chuck
4 T. raw rice
4 T. grated onion
2 T. catsup
1 egg
1 t. salt
½ t. pepper
1 large can tomatoes
1 can tomato soup
¼ c. white raisins
   Juice of 1 lemon
½ c. brown sugar
1 medium onion, sliced
½ t. salt

Cut a wedge from the core of the cabbage. Place in a large pot of boiling water, core side down. Simmer until the leaves separate. Put 12 large leaves back into the water for about a minute until slightly soft. Lift out and cut away the thick part of each leaf.

In a bowl mix ground chuck, rice, grated onion, catsup, egg, 1 teaspoon salt and the pepper. Put a twelfth of meat mixture on each leaf, fold in the sides and roll up. Mix tomatoes, tomato soup, lemon juice, sugar and remaining salt.

Line a shallow casserole with some shredded cabbage and onion slices. Spoon in half of the tomato mixture, then filled cabbage rolls. Cover with remaining shredded cabbage, onion slices and tomato mixture. Bake covered in a preheated 350° oven for 1 hour. Uncover, add raisins, baste and bake 2 more hours, basting occasionally. Makes 4 to 6 servings.

## LAMB PILAF

For a taste of the Middle East, throw caution to the winds and proceed as directed.

2 T. butter or margarine
3 lbs. boned lamb
1 large onion, sliced
½ t. cinnamon
½ t. freshly ground pepper
2 c. raw white rice
1 c. white raisins
2 t. salt
1 can consommé
2 c. water
¼ c. lemon juice
1 c. slivered almonds
3 T. snipped parsley

Cut lamb in 1-inch cubes. Melt butter and sauté lamb over high heat until brown. Remove lamb as it browns and drain on paper toweling. After all lamb is browned, lower heat to medium and sauté onion, cinnamon and pepper for 3 to 5 minutes.

In a buttered casserole, sprinkle about ½ cup rice to cover bottom. Make layers of rice, raisins, meat and onions. Repeat until all are used up. Sprinkle top with salt. Combine consommé and water and pour over the mixture in the casserole. Cover and bake in a preheated 400° oven 60 minutes. Remove cover, sprinkle with lemon juice and almonds and bake for 10 more minutes. Add parsley just before serving. Makes 8 to 10 servings.

## GIGOT À LA MOUTARDE

Leg of lamb roasted in the French manner will find its way to your table often after you've tried it.

1 6- to 8-lb. leg of lamb
½ c. Dijon mustard
2 T. soy sauce
1 t. rosemary or thyme
1 garlic clove, slivered
¼ t. powdered ginger
2 T. oil

Blend mustard, soy sauce, herbs and ginger in a bowl. Beat in oil to make a creamy mixture. Make 4 shallow slashes in the meat with a sharp knife and tuck into each a sliver of garlic. Brush lamb liberally with sauce and let stand for 1 to 2 hours. Roast on a rack in a preheated 350° oven for 1¼ to 1½ hours. Makes 4 to 6 servings.

## LAMB CHOPS À LA GRECQUE

Shoulder chops need help, and here is the way to make them tender and succulent.

4 to 6 shoulder lamb chops, round bone
1 1-lb. can whole tomatoes
1 onion, chopped
1 green pepper, cut in square chunks
1 t. salt
½ t. sugar
1 t. dried oregano
1 clove garlic, minced

Score fat around edges of chops to prevent curling. Brown both sides well under broiler. Drain off all fat. In the broiler pan, combine tomatoes, onion, green pepper, salt, sugar, oregano and garlic. Place chops on top and bake in a preheated 350° oven 30 to 45 minutes, until chops are tender.

Sliced zucchini may be added during the last 10 minutes of baking if desired. Makes 4 to 6 servings.

## GLAZED LAMB CHOPS

An unusual way to serve lamb, using the less expensive shoulder chops.

4 to 6 large shoulder lamb chops,
  ¾-inch thick
  Salt and pepper to taste
2 T. oil
½ t. curry powder
½ c. orange juice
2 T. lemon juice
4 T. honey
1 11-oz. can mandarin oranges, drained

Sprinkle chops with salt and pepper. Score fat around edges of chops to prevent curling. Brown both sides well under broiler. Drain off all fat. Place in oiled baking pan. Combine curry powder, orange juice, lemon juice and honey. Pour over chops and bake in a preheated 350° oven 30 to 45 minutes. Add oranges to sauce for last 5 minutes to warm them. Yield: 4 to 6 servings.

# POULTRY

## ROAST DUCK WITH ORANGE SAUCE

1 4- to 5-lb. duckling, cleaned
1 large whole onion, peeled
½ c. orange juice

Pull out all loose fat from cavity and from inside of neck. Place onion in cavity. Roast duck on a rack in a preheated 350° oven for 2½ to 3 hours. Prick skin with fork to drain fat. When bird begins to brown baste every 15 to 20 minutes with orange juice.

### SAUCE

1 T. duck drippings
1 c. orange juice
¼ c. orange peel, julienned
¼ c. currant jelly
¼ c. brown sugar
1½ T. cornstarch
   (dissolved in ¼ c. cold water)

Boil julienned orange peel 5 minutes, then drain. In a saucepan combine all ingredients and cook until thick and clear. Pour ¼ cup sauce over duck and serve remaining sauce at the table. Do not slice duck. Serve in quarters.

## CHICKEN COUNTRY CAPTAIN

1 frying chicken, cut up
½ c. flour
½ t. salt
⅛ t. pepper
¼ c. butter
1 medium onion, diced
½ green pepper, diced
1 clove garlic, minced
1½ t. curry powder
½ t. thyme
1 1-lb. can stewed tomatoes
½ c. currants
   Toasted slivered almonds

Dredge chicken in seasoned flour. Brown in butter. Remove. Sauté onion, green pepper and garlic in drippings until soft. Add curry powder and cook for 2 to 3 minutes. Add tomatoes, thyme and currants. Cook 2 to 3 minutes. Put chicken in baking dish. Pour sauce over chicken and bake at 350° for 45 minutes, or until chicken is tender. Garnish with almonds.

## CHICKEN ALMOND

With an Oriental touch, chicken quickly becomes exotic.

3 c. cooked chicken (4 double
   chicken breasts)
3 T. oil
2 c. celery, cut in ½-inch slices
2¼ c. chicken stock
3 T. soy sauce
4 T. cornstarch
1 t. sugar
½ c. water
2 cans Chinese vegetables
½ c. whole almonds
2 T. sherry
1 or 2 pkgs. frozen Chinese pea pods,
   thawed, drained and dried (optional)

Heat chicken in hot oil until golden brown. Add celery, chicken stock and soy sauce. Cook a few minutes. Mix together cornstarch, sugar and water. Add to chicken mixture and simmer until thickened. Add Chinese vegetables, almonds and sherry. Simmer just until mixture is heated through. If desired, add pea pods and stir into hot mixture. Do not overcook. Serve over Chinese noodles or rice. Serves 6 to 8.

## CHICKEN VERMOUTH

This recipe is economical and delicious as well as low in calories.

4 whole chicken breasts
¼ c. butter
1 clove garlic, minced
1 t. salt
¼ t. pepper
½ lb. mushrooms, sliced
1 T. lemon juice
¾ c. dry vermouth
¼ c. snipped parsley

Simmer chicken breasts in water to cover until tender enough to remove from bones. Sauté in butter. Add garlic, salt, pepper and lemon juice. Heap mushrooms on top, pour on vermouth, cover and cook for 20 to 30 minutes or until chicken is fork tender. Add a little more vermouth if needed. Sprinkle with parsley just before serving. Makes 6 servings.

## CURRIED CHICKEN, TURKEY OR LAMB

Create a sensation with a spicy, steaming bowl of curry and a bowl of fluffy rice surrounded by small bowls of assorted condiments. Have at least four condiments — salty, sweet, crunchy and spicy. Everyone will want to sprinkle some of each over the top of the curry.

5 T. butter
1 onion, chopped
2 tart apples, chopped
4 T. flour
2 t. curry powder
2 cans beef consommé
   (or chicken broth for chicken or turkey)
1 c. water
   Juice of 1 lemon
4 c. cooked, cubed lamb, chicken or turkey
   (leftovers may be used)
   Cooked rice

Melt 2 tablespoons of the butter and sauté onion and apples until tender. Add the rest of the butter and blend in the flour and curry powder. Stir in consommé, water and lemon juice, cook until slightly thickened. Add meat and simmer for 30 to 45 minutes. Cook ahead and reheat if desired. Serve with rice and assorted condiments, such as bacon cooked and crumbled (or bacon substitute), chutney (see accompaniments), coconut, chopped peanuts, slivered toasted almonds, snipped green onions, chopped hard-cooked egg, raisins, mandarin oranges, chopped green pepper. Makes 8 servings.

## CHICKEN ESPAÑOL

Señors and Señoritas will enjoy this Spanish cuisine.

    4 lbs. chicken, cut in pieces
    ¼ c. olive oil
    2 T. oil
    1 onion, chopped
    1 clove garlic, minced
    1 green pepper, cut in 1-inch cubes
    1 can tomato soup
    ½ c. pimiento stuffed olives, sliced
    ½ c. pitted black olives, sliced
    ½ lb. fresh mushrooms, sliced and sautéed
    ½ c. Burgundy wine

Heat ¼ cup olive oil in pan. Season chicken and sauté in oil until golden brown. Remove from pan. Add additional 2 tablespoons oil and sauté onion, garlic and green pepper. Add soup and olives and blend. Place chicken in sauce. Cover, bring to a boil and simmer 1½ hours or until tender. Add mushrooms and wine last 15 minutes of cooking time. This dish may be made in advance and wine and mushrooms added before reheating. Serve in a casserole or chafing dish. Yield: 6 to 8 servings.

## CHICKEN PHILIPPE

Chicken fit for a king or Bob, Bruce and Bill.

    ½ lb. mushrooms, sliced
    3 T. butter
    1 frying chicken, cut in pieces
    1 t. salt
    ½ t. pepper
    ½ c. salad oil
    1¼ c. rice, uncooked
    1 clove garlic, minced
    3 c. chicken broth
    1 jar white onions
      (or ½ pkg. frozen whole onions)
    ½ c. dry white wine
    ½ c. toasted slivered almonds

Sauté mushrooms in butter; remove from pan. Season chicken with salt and pepper; brown on all sides in oil. Remove chicken; lightly brown rice and garlic in remaining oil. Stir in 2 cups broth; turn into a large casserole. Arrange chicken, mushrooms and onions on rice. Mix remaining broth with wine; pour over all. Cover and bake in a preheated 350° oven 45 minutes. Uncover and bake 30 minutes longer. Top with almonds. Serves 4 to 6.

## COQ AU VIN

    ¼ lb. bacon, cut up
    2½- to 3½-lb. cut-up frying chicken
    ½ t. salt
    ⅛ t. pepper
    ¼ c. brandy
    3 c. Burgundy
    1 to 2 c. bouillon
    4 T. tomato paste
    2 cloves garlic
    ¼ t. thyme
    1 bay leaf
    1 pkg. frozen onions
    ½ lb. mushrooms
    2 to 3 T. butter

Simmer bacon 10 minutes in water. Drain, rinse in cold water and dry. Sauté slowly until lightly browned. Remove. Brown chicken in bacon fat. Season with salt and pepper. Return bacon to pan. Cover and cook 10 to 15 minutes. Uncover, add brandy and ignite. Shake pan until flames subside.

Pour Burgundy into pan. Add enough bouillon to cover chicken. Stir in tomato paste, garlic and seasonings. Bring to a simmer, cover and cook 30 minutes or until chicken is fork tender.

Sauté onions in butter until lightly browned. Remove from pan. Sauté mushrooms for a few minutes. When chicken is done, remove from pan and boil down sauce to about 2½ cups. Taste for seasoning. Skim fat. Return chicken, onions and mushrooms to sauce and heat through.

## CHICKEN ORIENTALE (LOW-CAL)

Chicken chicanery and a magic touch make this a delightful dish that is low in calories.

    1 to 2 frying chickens, quartered
      (removing skin is optional)
    ½ c. soy sauce
    2 cloves garlic, minced
    1 t. ginger
    2 T. oil
    ½ t. salt
    ¼ t. pepper
    1 T. sherry

Mix soy sauce, garlic, ginger, oil, salt, pepper and sherry. Pour over the chicken. If time allows, it can marinate all day in the refrigerator. Or it can be mixed and poured over the chicken just before baking in a preheated 350° oven for 1 hour and 30 minutes. It will be crispy and very brown.

## POULET À LA MARENGO

Chicken, the cook's best friend and a real budget buy, comes up smiling again.

1 broiler-fryer, cut in pieces
¼ c. oil
½ c. chopped onion
1 t. salt
⅛ t. pepper
¼ t. oregano, crushed
1 clove garlic, minced
2 tomatoes, peeled and quartered
½ c. dry white wine
1 3-oz. can sliced mushrooms
    Parsley

Brown chicken slowly in hot oil. Add onion; cook until onion is soft. Drain fat, season with salt and pepper. Add oregano, garlic, wine and broth drained from mushrooms. Scrape bottom of pan to loosen browned bits. Cover and cook over low heat until chicken is tender, about 35 minutes. Add tomatoes and mushrooms to chicken. Continue cooking for 5 minutes. Garnish with parsley. Makes 4 servings.

## CHICKEN DIVAN

A very special way to use leftover chicken or turkey.

1 lb. cooked asparagus spears or
    broccoli (fresh or frozen)
    Sliced cooked chicken or turkey
1 can cream of chicken or celery soup
¼ c. cream
½ c. dry Sauterne
½ c. grated parmesan cheese
1 T. butter, cut into dots
    Paprika

Place cooked vegetable on the bottom of a greased shallow, flat-bottomed casserole. Lay chicken slices on top, overlapping them. In a saucepan, mix soup, cream, wine and half of the cheese. Cook over low heat until smooth and well blended, stirring constantly. Pour sauce over the chicken, covering completely. Top with parmesan cheese, dot with butter, sprinkle lightly with paprika and bake in a preheated 450° oven until golden brown on top, about 15 minutes. Serves 4.

## HAWAIIAN CHICKEN

Say aloha to this Hawaiian chicken dish; you may want to go native.

    Chicken breasts or 1 fryer
¾ c. vinegar
1 c. sugar
2 T. cornstarch
1 T. mustard
1 T. Worcestershire sauce
1 13¼-oz. can pineapple chunks and juice
1 green pepper, cut in ¼-inch strips
1 tomato, quartered
2 T. sherry

Cut fryer in pieces to serve 4 to 6. Prepare sauce while chicken is baking. In a saucepan, stir vinegar into cornstarch and sugar and cook until clear. Then add mustard, Worcestershire sauce and pineapple juice, stirring until well blended. About 15 to 20 minutes before serving time, add pineapple chunks, green pepper, tomato and sauce to the chicken and broil on center rack in oven until chicken is glazed and hot. Five minutes before serving, stir in the sherry.

## SHERRIED CHICKEN RISOTTO

Everybody will want second helpings of this dish.

1¼ c. raw rice
1 can cream of mushroom soup
1 can cream of chicken soup
¼ c. melted butter or margarine
¼ c. dry sherry
10 to 12 pieces of chicken (legs,
    thighs and breasts)
½ c. slivered almonds
⅓ c. grated parmesan cheese

Lightly butter a 3-quart baking dish and sprinkle rice over the bottom. In a bowl combine soups, butter and sherry. Spread 1½ cups of soup mixture over the rice. Place chicken in single layer on top of soup. Spread the remaining soup mixture over chicken. Bake covered in a preheated 350° oven for 1 hour. Remove cover and bake 1 hour longer. Sprinkle with almonds and cheese the last 15 to 20 minutes of baking time. Makes 4 to 6 servings.

 # VEAL

## VEAL À LA FRANCAISE

Celebrate the happy marriage of veal, wine and herbs at your dinner table.

5 lbs. veal rump, boned and rolled
1 t. salt
¼ t. pepper
3 c. dry white wine
1 T. lemon-pepper marinade
1 clove garlic, slivered
1 bay leaf
½ t. rosemary
½ t. tarragon

Place meat in a large roasting pan. Blend seasonings into wine and pour around meat. Cover loosely with foil and bake in a preheated 350° oven for 2½ to 3 hours. Baste every 15 minutes and recover with foil. When meat is cooked, remove from oven and make the following sauce.

### SAUCE

2 c. meat juices (add wine if necessary)
2 lbs. mushrooms, washed and sliced
⅛ lb. butter or margarine
1 T. flour
¼ c. cold water

Sauté mushrooms in butter, drain and set aside. Skim fat from meat liquid. Blend flour with water, add meat juices, place in a saucepan and cook until slightly thickened, stirring constantly. Stir in mushrooms, pour sauce over veal in roasting pan, return to oven and cook 30 minutes longer. Serve sliced thin with sauce. Makes 8 to 10 servings.

## VEAL À LA BOLOGNESE

Veal chops reach their zenith by adding ham and cheese and this smooth sauce.

6 veal chops, steaks or cutlets
1 egg (beaten with 2 T. water)
1 c. bread crumbs
½ c. grated parmesan cheese
½ t. salt
  Black pepper, freshly ground
½ c. butter
6 slices of salami or cooked ham
1 c. milk
1 c. tomato sauce

Dip meat into egg mixture and then into bread crumbs which have been combined with 2 tablespoons of the cheese, the salt and the pepper. Sauté in butter for 10 minutes. Top meat with salami or ham and sprinkle with remaining cheese. Combine milk and tomato sauce and pour over meat. Cover and simmer for 25 minutes. Makes 6 servings.

> Wipe nonstick pans with a drop or two of oil after washing — never scour.

## VEAL LOUISA

A perfect dish for dinner or buffet supper. Serve in a chafing dish, along with a bowl of rice or noodles.

2 lbs. lean veal
1 t. paprika
1 t. salt
¼ t. pepper
3 T. flour
2 T. oil
2 T. butter
1 clove garlic, minced
½ onion, chopped fine
  (or 2 T. instant minced onion)
1 c. chicken broth or instant bouillon
½ c. Sauterne
½ to 1 c. sour cream

Cut veal into strips. Dredge in flour, paprika, salt and pepper. Sauté in butter and oil over medium heat until brown. Add garlic, onion, broth and wine. Cover and simmer gently for 20 minutes, until tender. Just before serving, stir in sour cream. Serve over rice or noodles. Makes 4 to 5 servings.

## VEAL VERMOUTH

Chill the wine and light the candles; it's as romantic as a night in Venice.

1½ lbs. thin veal steak
2 T. flour
¼ c. butter
1 clove garlic, minced
½ lb. mushrooms, sliced
½ t. salt
Dash of pepper
1 T. lemon juice
⅓ c. dry vermouth
2 T. snipped parsley

Flatten veal to ¼-inch thick. Cut into 2-inch squares and flour. Melt butter and sauté veal, a little at a time, until golden brown on both sides. Return all meat and the garlic to the skillet and heap mushrooms on top. Sprinkle with salt, pepper and lemon juice. Pour on vermouth, cover and cook over low heat for 20 minutes or until veal is fork tender. Add a little more vermouth if needed. Sprinkle with parsley just before serving. This dish can be prepared ahead and reheated in the oven. Serves 4.

 # PORK

## PORTUGUESE PORK TENDERLOIN

You will earn special commendations for tenderloin in this fragrant wine sauce.

- 2 lbs. pork tenderloin
- 2 T. flour
- 3 T. butter
- 1 onion, sliced
- 2/3 c. dry white wine
- 1/2 lb. sliced mushrooms
- 1/8 t. rosemary
- 2 T. lemon juice
- 2 T. parsley, chopped

Season flour with salt, pepper, paprika. Roll tenderloins in seasoned flour. Sauté in butter until golden brown. Add sliced onion and mushrooms, sauté for a minute or two. Add wine and rosemary. Cover and cook over low heat for 45 to 60 minutes, until tenderloins are done. Add lemon juice and parsley just before serving. Makes 4 to 6 servings.

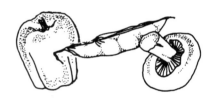

## SCALLOPED PORK CHOPS

A pork chop treated well can hold its own in any company.

- 6 to 8 pork chops
- 1 T. mustard
- 1 T. salad oil
- 4 to 6 medium potatoes, peeled and sliced thin
- 1 small onion, chopped
- 1 can cream of celery soup
- 1 soup can milk
- 1 to 2 t. salt
- 1/4 t. pepper
- 1/2 t. marjoram

Spread a little mustard on each chop and brown chops in oil. In a 2- to 3-quart casserole, arrange potatoes, onion and chops in layers. Mix soup, milk, salt, pepper and marjoram together and pour over potatoes and chops. Cover and bake in a preheated 350° oven for 1½ to 2 hours. Makes 4 to 6 servings.

## CASSOULET

A traditional cassoulet calls for a pork roast, a lamb roast, homemade sausage and three days of roasting, cooking and blending. This one will simmer along in your electric frying pan and be ready in about an hour.

- 12 large uncooked Italian sausages
- 2 pkgs. frozen lima beans, thawed
- 3 fresh tomatoes (or 1 can)
- 1 large onion, chopped
- 2 cloves garlic, minced
  Salt and pepper to taste
- 1 bay leaf
- 1/2 t. sweet basil
- 2 t. sugar
- 1/3 c. chicken broth
- 5 T. chopped parsley
- 1 large bottle dry vermouth (or dry white wine)

Put sausages in a cold frying pan. Pour wine until it comes halfway up the sausages. Cover and steam for about 15 minutes. Remove cover and sauté the sausages until brown. Remove to platter.

Using a little of the sausage fat, sauté onion and garlic until golden. Add tomatoes, bay leaf, pepper, basil and sugar; simmer 3 minutes. Add chicken broth and ½ cup wine. Then add lima beans, sausages and 3 tablespoons of the parsley. Cover and cook for 45 minutes. Add salt and pepper to taste. Sprinkle with remaining parsley and serve. Makes 6 to 8 servings.

## SPARERIBS ALOHA

A new taste sensation for your family and friends.

- 3 lbs. meaty spareribs
- 1 13¼-oz. can pineapple chunks with juice
- 1 green pepper, cut into 1-inch pieces
- 3 T. brown sugar
- 1 T. cornstarch
- 3 T. vinegar
- 1 t. salt
- 1/4 c. soy sauce
- 3 pieces preserved ginger, slivered

Cut spareribs into 2 or 3 rib sections and brown in a 350° oven for 1 hour, pouring off excess fat frequently. Add pineapple, juice and green pepper. Blend brown sugar, cornstarch, vinegar, salt and soy sauce; add ginger. Pour over ribs and bake for another 30 minutes, basting frequently. Serves 3 to 4.

## FILLET OF SOLE VERONIQUE

An epicure's delight.

- 1 lb. sole or flounder fillets
  Salt
- 1 T. lime juice
- 1 t. dried parsley
- ¼ t. tarragon
- ½ clove garlic, minced
- ¾ c. white wine
- ¼ lb. seedless green grapes
- 1½ T. butter
- 1 T. flour
- 2 T. orange juice

Sprinkle fish fillets lightly with salt and lime juice. Place in lightly greased skillet. Sprinkle with parsley, tarragon and garlic. Add wine and simmer 12 to 15 minutes until fish flake easily and look milky white, not transparent. Add grapes the last 5 minutes. Remove from heat but keep warm on a separate platter.

In the original skillet, melt butter with remaining juices and blend in flour until smooth. Add orange juice and cook, stirring until mixture thickens. Add more wine if desired. Pour sauce over fillets. Serves 3 to 4.

## POISSONS EN COQUILLE

- 2 lbs. fish fillets, cut in ½ x 2-inch strips
- 2 large onions, sliced
- ½ lb. fresh mushrooms, sliced
- 1 clove garlic, minced
- ¼ lb. butter
- 1½ t. salt
- ¼ t. white pepper
- 1 c. sour cream
- 2 t. Worcestershire sauce
- 1 t. mustard
  Buttered bread crumbs
  (or cooked egg noodles)
  Parsley to garnish

Sauté onions and mushrooms in half of the butter. Add garlic, cook for 1 minute. Remove from pan. Sauté fish until done in remainder of the butter. Return onions and mushrooms to pan. Blend seasonings with sour cream and stir gently into fish. Heat thoroughly. Serve in individual ramekins with toasted, buttered crumb topping or on a platter with cooked buttered noodles. Garnish with parsley. Makes 4 to 6 servings.

## FILLET OF SOLE FLORENTINE

Vary your fish repertoire. Top the delicate sole with creamy spinach.

- 2 lbs. sole or turbot fillets
- 2 T. butter or margarine, cut into dots
- ½ t. salt
- 2 10-oz. pkgs. frozen chopped spinach, cooked and drained
- 1 can cream of mushroom soup
- 3 T. sherry
- 1 T. butter or margarine, melted
- 3 T. dry bread crumbs
- 2 T. grated parmesan cheese

Wash, drain and dry the fish fillets. Arrange in a baking dish and dot with the butter or margarine. Sprinkle with salt, cover the dish with foil and bake in a preheated 350° oven for 15 minutes. Remove from oven and drain liquid.

Spread cooked spinach over the top of the fish. Blend soup with sherry and pour over all. Mix bread crumbs with melted butter and cheese and sprinkle over top. Bake uncovered for 20 minutes. Yield: 6 to 8 servings.

## FILLET OF HADDOCK MARGUERY

The Friday fish fry, try it baked any day of the week.

- 2 lbs. fresh or frozen haddock, sole or turbot fillets, thawed and drained
- 1 can cream of celery or shrimp soup
- 1 can shrimp, washed and drained (optional)
- ¼ c. butter or margarine, melted
- ½ t. grated onion
- ½ t. Worcestershire sauce
- ¼ t. garlic salt
- 1 T. sherry
- 1¼ c. crushed rich crackers

Place fish fillets in a greased 13 x 9 x 2-inch baking dish. Combine soup and sherry. Spread fillets with soup and shrimp. Bake in a preheated 375° oven for 20 minutes. Combine butter and seasonings, mix with crumbs and sprinkle over fish. Bake 10 minutes longer. Serves 6 to 8.

## SHRIMP NEWBURG

Delicate, rich and creamy.

   4 T. butter
   4 T. flour
  ½ t. salt
     Dash of pepper, freshly ground
   2 c. milk
   2 egg yolks, slightly beaten
1½ lbs. cooked shrimp
  ¼ c. sherry

Melt butter over low heat. Add flour, salt and pepper slowly, stirring constantly until smooth. Add the milk slowly, stirring constantly, and cook until thickened. Add a little of the hot milk mixture to the slightly beaten egg yolks, then return them to the milk. Stir and cook about 2 minutes. Add shrimp and heat thoroughly (do not boil). Add sherry, stir well and serve on hot toast points or in individual ramekins. Makes 4 servings.

## SHRIMP AND CRABMEAT SUPREME

A quick seafood delight! Out of the freezer and onto the table in half an hour.

    1 lb. frozen shrimp
    1 6-oz. pkg. frozen crabmeat
    1 pkg. white sauce mix
 1⅓ c. water
    ¼ c. white wine
    2 T. butter
 1½ c. coarse bread crumbs
    ¼ t. paprika
      Dash of cayenne pepper

Cook shrimp. Drain crabmeat. Add sauce mix to water and bring to a boil. Simmer 1 minute. Add cayenne pepper. Add wine, butter, shrimp and crabmeat. Pour into baking dish. Sprinkle crumbs and paprika over the top. Bake in a preheated 350° oven for 15 minutes. Makes 2 to 4 servings.

## LOBSTER THERMIDOR

Try this when you're in the mood to splurge, or trim the food budget by using poached cod, haddock or pollock in place of lobster.

    ¼ c. butter, melted
    ½ c. flour
    1 t. salt
      Pinch of cayenne pepper
    ¼ t. dry mustard
 2½ c. milk
    ½ lb. fresh mushrooms, sliced
    ¼ c. butter
    4 c. cooked lobster (bite-sized pieces)
    2 T. dry sherry
    ⅓ c. grated parmesan cheese

To the melted butter, add flour, salt, cayenne and mustard, stirring constantly until smooth. Add the milk slowly, stirring constantly. Cook until thickened. Remove from heat. Sauté the mushrooms in the ¼ cup butter. Add mushrooms, lobster and sherry to the sauce. Mix well and pour into a buttered casserole. Sprinkle the top with parmesan cheese. Bake in a preheated 400° oven about 15 minutes until bubbly. Makes 6 to 8 servings, but recipe may be cut in half.

Variation: Add ¼ to ½ cup grated Swiss cheese to cream sauce.

## SHRIMP CURRY

Choose at least four of the condiments listed below. You should have a combination of sweet, crispy, salty and tangy to complement the distinctive flavor of the curry.

    1 lb. cooked, cleaned shrimp
    ¼ c. melted butter
    ¼ c. flour
    ½ t. salt
 1½ c. milk
    1 t. curry powder
    3 T. catsup
    ¼ c. sherry
      Dash of paprika

Blend flour, salt and melted butter over medium heat until smooth. Slowly stir in milk. Cook, stirring gently, until thickened. Blend in catsup and curry powder. Add shrimp and heat through. Just before serving, stir in sherry and sprinkle with paprika. Serve over hot rice with assorted condiments, such as chopped hard-cooked egg, raisins, crumbled bacon or bacon substitute, coconut, snipped green onions, chopped peanuts or chutney. Serves 4.

## SHRIMP CREOLE

Creole is from New Orleans, where seafood is an everyday ingredient in their cuisine. This dish is so quick and easy you will want to serve it frequently.

    ⅔ c. onion, chopped
    ½ c. green pepper, chopped
    ½ c. celery, chopped
    2 T. butter
    1 large can tomatoes
    1 8-oz. can tomato sauce
    2 cloves garlic, minced
    2 bay leaves
    1 t. salt
    ¼ t. pepper
    ½ t. oregano
      Celery salt to taste
 1½ lbs. shrimp, cooked

Sauté onions, green pepper, celery in butter. Add tomatoes, tomato sauce and seasonings and simmer for about 40 minutes. Add cooked shrimp just before serving. Serve over cooked rice. Yield: 4 to 6 servings.

Note: Chicken and pork chops are delicious when baked in this sauce at 350° for 1 hour.

## SALMON DIABLE

Stretch a can of salmon into a luncheon dish or appetizer.

½ c. sour cream
¼ c. mayonnaise
¼ c. sherry
1 T. lemon juice
1 T. Worcestershire sauce
½ t. dry mustard
2 eggs, slightly beaten
⅛ t. tabasco
¼ c. chopped celery (optional)
1 1-lb. can salmon, drained and flaked
⅓ c. cracker crumbs
¼ c. snipped parsley
1 T. snipped chives, fresh or frozen
Salt and pepper to taste
Paprika
Lemon slices

Mix together sour cream, mayonnaise, sherry, lemon juice, Worcestershire sauce, mustard, celery, eggs and tabasco. Pour over the salmon, cracker crumbs, parsley, chives, salt and pepper. Stir gently until well blended. Spoon into 6 baking shells or a baking dish. Sprinkle with paprika and bake in a preheated 350° oven for 30 minutes. Garnish with lemon slices. Serve with the following sauce. Serves 4.

### SAUCE

1 c. sour cream
1 t. mustard
1 t. horseradish
¼ t. salt
1 T. snipped chives

Combine and stir.

## TUNA PÂTÉ

Tuna, the perennial sandwich filling, takes on a new look.

2 7-oz. cans water-packed tuna fish, drained and flaked
1 8-oz. pkg. cream cheese, softened
1 T. grated onion
3 T. chili sauce
1 t. Worcestershire sauce
2 T. snipped parsley
2 T. dry sherry

Blend together cream cheese, onion, chili sauce, Worcestershire sauce and parsley. Add tuna fish and sherry and mix well. Add salt to taste. Heap in a bowl or make into a ball. Serve with raw relishes or crisp crackers.

## BOUILLABAISSE

This is an adaptation of a traditional fisherman's dish into which whatever was not sold of the day's catch was put into a stew. The idea is to have a variety of seafoods; the choice is yours. Substitutions are in order if you don't care for, or can't get, one of the listed seafoods or fish. It makes a complete meal.

⅓ c. olive oil
1 clove garlic, minced
2 medium onions, sliced
2 1-lb. cans tomatoes
2 lbs. frozen flounder fillets, thawed and cut into fingers
1 7½-oz. can crabmeat, drained and cartilage removed ( or ½ lb. fresh)
1 7½-oz. can chopped clams and juice
1 1-lb. pkg. frozen shrimp, thawed
1 t. bouillon crystals
1 bay leaf
½ c. chopped pimiento
¼ c. dried parsley flakes
½ t. thyme
½ t. saffron
1 c. dry white wine

Sauté onions and garlic in olive oil until golden. Add tomatoes, flounder, crabmeat, clams, shrimp, bouillon crystals and bay leaf. Simmer 15 to 20 minutes. Add pimiento, parsley flakes, thyme, saffron and wine. Turn heat to low, cover, and let stand for about 10 minutes to absorb flavors. Makes 8 to 10 servings.

## CLAMS FLORENTINE EN COQUILLE

A unique appetizer or a seafaring supper.

4 pkgs. frozen chopped spinach
1 can cream of mushroom soup
2 eggs, lightly beaten
2 cans minced clams, drained
4 T. butter, cut in dots
½ t. salt
¼ t. pepper
¼ c. sliced almonds or pine nuts (or ½ c. buttered bread crumbs)

Cook spinach until barely done. If thawed, don't cook. Drain well. Add soup, eggs, clams, butter, salt and pepper. Mix well and spoon into lightly greased seashells or ramekins. Sprinkle with nuts or bread crumbs. Bake in a preheated 350° oven for 30 to 40 minutes. Makes 10 to 12 servings.

## ÉPINARDS À LA CRÈME

This delightfully different combination of vegetables and creamy sauce goes well with baked or broiled fish.

2 pkgs. frozen chopped spinach
1 small onion, chopped fine
1 T. butter or margarine
1 T. flour
½ c. milk (or half-and-half)
1 jar small whole onions (or ½ pkg. frozen)
½ c. beef bouillon
1 t. salt
   Pinch of pepper
   Pinch of nutmeg

Cook spinach lightly, drain well. Sauté onion in butter until soft. Blend in flour and then stir in milk, bouillon, salt, pepper and nutmeg. Stir until mixture is creamy. Add spinach and remove from heat. Place whole onions in a lightly greased baking dish, pour spinach mixture over the onions and bake in a preheated 325° oven for about 20 minutes. Serves 8.

## ZUCCHINI PARMESAN

This dish is ready to serve in the same amount of time it takes to prepare a package of frozen vegetables. Everyone will think you've cooked for hours.

1 onion, sliced
¼ c. butter, margarine or oil
4 to 6 zucchini
¼ t. salt
⅛ t. pepper
½ c. grated parmesan cheese

Sauté onion in butter, margarine or oil until soft. Add zucchini (scrubbed and cut into ¼-inch rounds), salt and pepper and cook, tossing lightly, for about 5 minutes. Add cheese just before serving and toss lightly to coat well. Makes 4 servings.

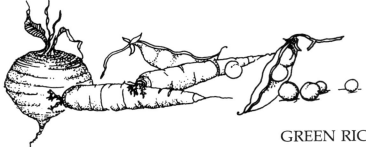

## BROCCOLI SOUFFLÉ

This is the soufflé of your dreams, with nothing to rise or fall. It will keep its shape very nicely until you are ready to serve it. (Turn the oven down to 300° while it waits.)

2 10-oz. pkgs. frozen chopped broccoli
   or spinach
½ c. chicken broth
2 c. well-drained cottage cheese
½ c. grated parmesan cheese
2 eggs, beaten
1 t. minced onion
1 t. salt

Cook the broccoli or spinach in chicken broth and drain well. Combine cheeses, eggs, onion and salt. Gently mix in the broccoli or spinach. Bake in a greased 2½-quart casserole in a preheated 350° oven about 30 minutes, or until a knife inserted in the center comes out clean. Makes 8 servings.

## GREEN RICE RING

A lovely container for shrimp Creole but delicious with beef or fowl, too. Fill the center with glazed carrots if desired.

3 c. cooked white rice
3 egg yolks, beaten
1 c. cream
1 t. salt
¼ t. pepper
1 c. minced parsley
1 c. minced green pepper
¼ c. minced onion
¼ lb. grated American or cheddar cheese
3 egg whites

Combine egg yolks, cream, salt, pepper, parsley, green pepper and onion. Stir in the cooked rice and cheese. Beat egg whites until stiff but not dry and fold into the rice mixture. Grease a 3-quart ring mold generously, pour in rice mixture and bake in a pan of hot water in a preheated 350° oven about 45 minutes, or until a knife inserted in the center comes out clean. Serves 10 to 12.

## GHIVETCH

It is important to have a variety of shapes, colors and flavors in this beautiful vegetable mélange. Vary the amounts to suit your taste. Substitute eggplant for zucchini, cabbage for celery or add a sliced turnip. Increase the servings by adding another carrot, potato or tomato.

2 medium carrots, sliced thin
2 small potatoes, cubed
4 medium tomatoes, quartered
1 Bermuda onion, sliced
1 small head cauliflower (small flowers)
½ green pepper, julienne strips
½ sweet red pepper, julienne strips
½ pkg. frozen green peas, thawed
1 c. fresh green beans, sliced
1 rib celery, sliced
3 small zucchini, sliced
1 c. beef bouillon
1 c. olive oil
1 clove garlic, minced
2 t. salt
½ bay leaf, crumbled
½ t. savory
¼ t. tarragon

Put all of the vegetables in an ungreased, shallow, 11 x 13-inch casserole dish. Heat bouillon, oil, garlic, salt, bay leaf, savory and tarragon to boiling and pour over vegetables. Cover casserole with heavy foil. Bake in a preheated 350° oven until tender, about 1 hour. The vegetables should be crisp and colorful. Makes 8 to 10 servings.

## ZUCCHINI AU GRATIN

Zucchini with a surprise. A touch of tomato, topped with bubbly melted cheese, makes this deliciously different.

    4 T. oil
    4 zucchini
    1 clove garlic, minced
    1 small onion, chopped
    ¼ t. pepper, freshly ground
    ½ t. salt
    2 T. grated parmesan cheese
    ¼ c. tomato sauce or paste
    2 to 3 slices processed Swiss cheese

Heat oil in a skillet. Add zucchini (scrubbed and cut into ¼-inch rounds), garlic and onion and sauté for 5 minutes. Add pepper, salt and parmesan cheese and toss lightly. Place in a greased 1-quart casserole and brush with tomato sauce or paste. Cover with slices of Swiss cheese and bake in a preheated 350° oven about 15 to 20 minutes until the cheese melts and is bubbly. Makes 4 servings.

## SPINACH FLORENTINE

Everyone will eat spinach cooked in this unusual way.

    1 8-oz. pkg. wide noodles
    1 onion, chopped fine
    ½ c. butter
    2 10-oz. pkgs. chopped spinach,
      thawed and drained
    1 t. salt
    3 eggs, slightly beaten
    1 c. sour cream (or sour cream substitute)

Cook noodles in salted water until barely tender, then drain. Sauté onion in butter. Combine all ingredients and place in a well-greased 6-cup ring mold. Place mold in pan of hot water and bake in a 350° oven 45 minutes. Unmold and serve hot. Makes 6 to 8 servings.

Cold cheese grates easily. It may be grated in advance, rewrapped and returned to the refrigerator until needed.

## CHINESE VEGETABLES

The Chinese call this method of cooking vegetables "stir-frying." Done very quickly and with a minimum of liquid, it permits the vegetables to remain tender, crisp and colorful. The flavor is enhanced by the broth, soy sauce and a touch of sugar.

    1 lb. fresh green beans, carrots, cauliflower,
      broccoli or Brussels sprouts
    3 T. oil
    1 T. soy sauce
    ½ t. sugar
    ¼ c. chicken broth

Wash and slice vegetables. Heat oil in large skillet. Add vegetables and toss until coated with oil. Add soy sauce, sugar and broth. Cover skillet, reduce heat, steam for 8 to 10 minutes, shaking the pan occasionally to "stir" the vegetables. Serve immediately. Serves 4 to 6.

## CHINESE FRIED RICE

"May your rice never burn" is a Chinese New Year's greeting that means "Good Luck." When cooking fried rice you will have good luck if you keep stirring to prevent sticking. Fried rice is very tasty and well worth the effort. It is also a good way to use leftovers.

    3 c. cooked cold rice
    3 T. oil
    1 c. cooked chicken, shrimp or
      leftover meat
    2 eggs, slightly beaten
    ¾ t. salt
    ½ t. pepper
    2 T. soy sauce
    2 green onions, snipped

Heat oil in deep frying pan. Add meat or fish and cook 1 minute. Add eggs, salt and pepper and cook, stirring constantly, until well mixed. Add rice and soy sauce and cook, stirring constantly, for about 5 minutes, until rice is thoroughly heated. Garnish with green onions. Yield: 4 to 6 servings.

## VEGETABLES VINAIGRETTE

Everyone will enjoy these vegetables marinated with a touch of dill. Heaped on a lettuce-lined platter, they are a picture in shades of green and white.

⅔ c. salad oil
⅓ c. tarragon vinegar
1 t. sugar
1 t. salt
¼ t. tabasco
1 T. dried dill
2 T. snipped parsley
1 T. snipped chives
½ lb. fresh mushrooms, sliced
2 c. raw cauliflower buds
1 can artichoke hearts, drained
1 1-lb. can whole green beans, drained

Combine salad oil, vinegar, sugar, salt, tabasco, dill, parsley and chives and mix until thoroughly blended. Pour over vegetables and marinate in the refrigerator at least 3 hours before serving. This vegetable dish improves with age and will keep for several days in the refrigerator. Makes 12 servings.

## HOT WINE SAUCE FOR VEGETABLES

Dress up an ordinary package of frozen vegetables with this easy last-minute sauce and you will have something extraordinary.

1 T. minced onion
¼ c. dry Sauterne
2 T. chopped parsley
1 T. lemon juice
¾ c. mayonnaise
    Asparagus, broccoli, green beans or
    cauliflower, cooked

Combine onion, wine, parsley, lemon juice and mayonnaise in the top of a double boiler and heat over hot, not boiling, water. Serve over one of the above vegetables. Makes about 1 cup. Serves 4.

## POTATO PANCAKES

Crisp, lacy potato pancakes go well with beef and fowl as well as with breakfast ham and eggs.

2 c. raw grated potatoes
2 whole eggs, beaten
1 onion, grated
1½ t. salt
2 T. flour

Peel large potatoes and soak in cold water several hours. Grate potatoes and drain. (Grate in an electric blender if desired.) Add grated onion and beaten eggs, stir in salt and flour. Drop batter by spoonful onto a hot, well-greased frying pan or griddle. Turn to brown other side. Serve hot with applesauce or sour cream. Made in a miniature size they are delightful for appetizers. Keep hot on a warming tray, serve with cold sour cream. Makes 20 to 22 pancakes or 4 dozen miniatures.

---

Parsley will keep fresh and crisp if stored in a covered jar in the refrigerator.

---

## CORN PUDDING

This is a favorite with youngsters. Omit the green pepper and pimiento if desired. However, they add to both the flavor and the appearance of this pudding.

1 1-lb. can creamed corn
3 eggs, slightly beaten
½ t. salt
¼ t. pepper
1 T. sugar
¼ t. dry mustard
2 T. minced onion
½ c. green pepper, chopped
½ c. pimiento, chopped
1 c. coarse cracker crumbs
1 c. milk
2 T. butter, cut into dots

Combine all ingredients except butter. Pour into a greased casserole and dot with butter. Bake in a preheated 350° oven for 45 minutes to 1 hour, until a knife inserted into the center comes out clean. Makes 4 to 6 servings.

## TOMATOES À LA PROVENCALE

A handsome garnish for a roast or fowl, prepare this recipe in the morning and refrigerate until you are ready to bake it.

      12 tomatoes
      ¼ lb. butter or margarine
       1 c. chopped onion
       1 clove garlic, minced
    1½ c. fine dry bread crumbs
      ½ c. fresh parsley, snipped
       2 t. basil
       1 t. thyme
      ½ t. salt
      ¼ t. pepper, freshly ground

Cut a thin slice off the stem end of the tomatoes and cut out a wedge-shaped piece halfway down the tomato. Gently squeeze out the juice and remove the seeds, trying not to break shells. Melt butter in a skillet and cook onion and garlic until soft. Remove pan from heat and stir in crumbs, parsley, basil, thyme, salt and pepper. Spoon this mixture into the tomatoes, then place tomatoes in a shallow baking dish. Bake in a preheated 350° oven about 20 minutes until the filling is lightly browned and the tomatoes are tender. Makes 12 servings.

## EGGPLANT MAURICE

Never liked eggplant? We think you will change your mind.

      1 small eggplant, cubed
      1 1-lb. can tomatoes, drained
      1 green pepper, chopped
      1 medium onion, sliced thin
      ½ lb. cheddar cheese, shredded
      1 T. sugar
      1 t. salt
      ¼ t. pepper
      ½ t. garlic salt

Mix together sugar, salt, pepper and garlic salt. Set aside. Place a layer of eggplant in a greased casserole. Add a layer of tomatoes and some of the chopped green pepper and onion. Sprinkle lightly with the mixed seasonings. Add a layer of cheese. Repeat layers until casserole is filled, ending with the cheese. There is great shrinkage, so force the cover down over the high mound of vegetables. Cover and bake in a preheated 400° oven 20 minutes. Remove cover, reduce heat to 350° and continue baking for another 30 minutes. Serves 6.

## CARROT RING

Everyone will like carrots when they are artfully disguised in a carrot ring. It tastes like cake.

      ¾ c. soft shortening
      ¼ c. brown sugar
      1 egg
      ½ t. salt
      1 t. baking powder
      1 t. baking soda
    1¼ c. sifted flour
      1 c. grated carrots
      1 T. water
      1 T. lemon juice

Cream shortening and sugar until fluffy. Beat in egg. Combine salt, baking powder, baking soda and flour and add to mixture. Blend in carrots, water and lemon juice. Stir well and place in a greased 1½-quart ring mold. Bake in a preheated 350° oven 45 minutes. Serves 6.

This recipe may be doubled and baked in a 3-quart ring mold which will serve 12. Fill the center of the mold with cooked, drained peas if desired.

## RATATOUILLE

This versatile French vegetable casserole is delicious hot or cold. Prepare the day before, as it improves with age.

      ¼ c. olive oil
      1 clove garlic, minced
      2 onions, sliced thin
      2 green peppers, seeded and sliced
         into strips
      1 eggplant, peeled and cubed
      5 small zucchini, cut into ½-inch slices
      5 tomatoes, quartered
      1 t. salt
      1 t. thyme
      ⅛ t. pepper, freshly ground
      1 t. olive oil

Heat ¼ cup olive oil in a 2-quart saucepan. Add garlic and onions and cook 5 minutes over medium heat until the onions are transparent. Add the vegetables in layers, sprinkling each layer with salt, pepper and thyme. Sprinkle 1 teaspoon olive oil over the top. Simmer, covered, over low heat for 30 to 35 minutes. Remove cover and simmer for 10 more minutes to reduce the sauce. Yield: 6 to 8 servings.

## SWEET POTATOES IN ORANGE CUPS

Sweet potatoes are a natural with fowl or pork. Heaped into orange cups, they add a festive touch to any dinner.

6 yams or sweet potatoes
2 T. butter
¼ c. brown sugar
½ c. orange juice
12 orange cups

Scrub sweet potatoes and cook in a covered saucepan in a small amount of water until very tender. Remove skins and mash until smooth. Add butter, sugar and enough orange juice to give them the consistency of mashed potatoes. Heap into the prepared orange cups. Decorate tops with a marshmallow or maraschino cherry.

Sweet potatoes may be kept hot over simmering water and placed in orange cups just before serving. Or they may be filled and kept in a 300° oven 30 minutes. Makes 12 cups.

### ORANGE CUPS

Trace a line around the center of 6 oranges. Insert a small-bladed, pointed knife into the center of the orange at an angle to make one side of a point. Remove knife; insert to make opposite side of point. Continue around the orange, following the line to make halves equal sizes. Pull apart and scoop the fruit out of each half. You will have two shells with a picot edge. These cups may also be filled with cranberry relish.

## CURRIED YAMS AND FRUIT

A touch of curry powder turns ordinary canned fruit into a gourmet treat. The yams are optional.

⅓ c. butter
⅓ c. brown sugar
1 to 2 T. curry powder
1 1-lb. can pear halves
1 1-lb. can peach halves
1 1-lb. can pineapple slices
1 1-lb. can apricot halves
2 1-lb. cans yams or sweet potatoes (optional)

Melt butter, add brown sugar and curry powder and mix well. Drain fruits and yams and arrange in a 2½-quart casserole. Top with curry mixture. Bake 1 hour in a preheated 325° oven. Yield: 10 to 12 servings.

## MARINATED CARROTS

A lively change from the usual carrot sticks, Marinated Carrots keep for weeks in the refrigerator.

8 to 10 medium carrots, cut into sticks
¼ c. olive or salad oil
1½ T. cider vinegar
1 T. chopped green pepper
½ t. dry mustard
1 t. paprika
1 small clove garlic, minced
1 T. chopped green onion, chives or instant minced onion
1 t. salt
⅛ t. pepper
½ t. basil
1 T. lemon juice

Cook carrot sticks in 1 inch of boiling, salted water for 5 minutes. Drain. Combine the remaining ingredients, mix well and pour over the carrots. Refrigerate for at least 1 hour and serve cold.

## HOT FRUIT MEDLEY

Hot fruit compote goes well with beef or fowl, and also makes a delightful dessert.

12 dried macaroons, crumbled
4 large cans fruit: peach, pear, or apricot halves, pineapple slices, cherries
½ c. slivered almonds
¼ c. brown sugar
½ c. sherry
¼ c. melted butter

Butter a 2½-quart casserole. Cover the bottom with macaroon crumbs, then alternate layers of fruit and macaroons, finishing with macaroons. Sprinkle with sherry, brown sugar and almonds. Bake in a preheated 350° oven for 30 minutes. Add melted butter. Serve hot. Serves 8.

## SPICED PEACHES

A little competition for Grandma's recipe.

1 large can peach halves
½ c. sugar
½ c. peach juice
¼ c. vinegar
8 to 10 whole cloves
1 stick cinnamon

Combine sugar, juice, vinegar and spices. Bring to a boil and simmer 10 minutes. Add the fruit and heat thoroughly. Remove to a flat refrigerator dish. Be sure all fruit is covered with the syrup. Allow to stand refrigerated overnight.

# MOLDS

## CRANBERRY MOLD

A tradition at holiday dinners, here is one way to serve cranberries.

2 pkgs. cherry gelatin
2 c. boiling water
1 c. pineapple juice (plus water)
1 lb. fresh cranberries
1 orange
1 c. sugar
1 7-oz. can crushed pineapple, drained
¼ c. chopped nuts (optional)

Dissolve gelatin in boiling water, add pineapple juice plus water. Stir and chill until of jelly-like consistency. Coarsely grind cranberries and orange. Drain and discard liquid. Add sugar and let stand for 10 minutes. Add crushed pineapple and nuts and stir into semiset gelatin. Spoon into lightly oiled 6-cup mold and refrigerate until firm. Serves 10 to 12.

Note: 1 16-oz. can whole cranberry sauce may be substituted for fresh berries. Omit sugar.

## TOMATO ASPIC

Pretty and peppy with shrimp, crabmeat, chicken or tuna salad.

4 c. tomato juice
1 bay leaf
⅛ t. pepper
1 small onion, sliced
1 T. parsley
1 T. celery leaves
1 t. salt
1 clove garlic
1 t. sugar
2 T. lemon juice
3 T. unflavored gelatin (dissolved in
   ½ c. cold water)

Simmer all ingredients except lemon juice and gelatin for 15 minutes. Strain and pour into lemon juice and gelatin mixture. Stir until dissolved. Cool, then pour into a lightly oiled 6-cup mold. Chill until firm. Yield: 10 to 12 servings.

## EGG SALAD MOLD

A fix-ahead winner, serve as an hors d'oeuvre, appetizer or luncheon entrée.

12 hard-cooked eggs, chopped
½ c. chopped celery
½ c. chopped green pepper
2 t. grated onion
¼ t. white pepper
½ t. Worcestershire sauce
1 snipped green onion
1 c. mayonnaise
2 t. salt
1½ envelopes unflavored gelatin
   (dissolved in ¼ c. cold water)
¾ c. hot water

Combine all ingredients. Pour into a greased 6-cup mold. Chill until firm. Unmold and serve with bread rounds or crackers. Serve with shrimp sauce or decorate with black caviar if desired.

### SHRIMP SAUCE

½ c. mayonnaise
1 t. chili sauce
1 can small shrimp, washed
   and drained

Stir together all ingredients and chill until needed. Makes 12 servings.

## CUCUMBER RING

Put summer on your luncheon table — spring, fall or winter.

1 envelope unflavored gelatin
½ c. cold water
½ t. salt
4 c. creamed cottage cheese
2 3-oz. pkgs. cream cheese, softened
½ c. mayonnaise
1 medium cucumber, pared, seeded
   and grated
1 green onion, snipped
⅔ c. celery, finely chopped

Soften gelatin in cold water. Add salt. Heat and stir over low heat until gelatin is dissolved. Beat cheeses together; add mayonnaise and gelatin. Stir in cucumber, onion and celery. Pour into a lightly oiled 6-cup ring mold. Chill 6 to 8 hours or overnight. Garnish with cherry tomatoes and radishes.

## SALMON MOUSSE

Use a slice of olive for an eye and the fish will look like a whole poached salmon, swimming on a sea of endive. Serve as an appetizer or luncheon entrée.

1 can tomato soup
1 large pkg. cream cheese, softened
2 T. unflavored gelatin
  (dissolved in ¼ c. cold water)
1 large can salmon, drained and flaked
1 c. mayonnaise
1 green pepper, finely chopped
1 c. celery, chopped
1 small onion, grated
1 T. Worcestershire sauce
½ t. salt
¼ t. white pepper

Heat soup and cream cheese over low heat until cheese dissolves. Add softened gelatin and stir until well blended. Add remaining ingredients and mix well. Place in a well-greased fish mold and chill overnight in the refrigerator. Unmold on a bed of endive or leaf lettuce. Serve with Dill Sauce.

### DILL SAUCE

2 c. sour cream (or sour half-and-half)
½ t. salt
¼ t. pepper
1 T. chopped fresh dill (or 1½ t. dried dill)
2 T. snipped chives or green onions
¾ c. coarsely chopped cucumber,
  drained well

Mix all ingredients and chill before serving. Serves 12.

## ORANGE SHERBET MOLD

Tastes like summer sunshine!

2 3-oz. pkgs. orange gelatin
2 c. boiling water
⅓ c. lemon juice
1 pt. orange sherbet, softened
1 can mandarin oranges, drained
1 7-oz. can crushed pineapple, drained
  (save juice)

Dissolve gelatin in boiling water. Cool and add lemon and pineapple juices. Chill until of jelly-like consistency. Beat in softened sherbet, fold in oranges and pineapple. Place in a lightly oiled 6-cup mold and refrigerate until firm. Unmold and decorate with clusters of grapes. Yield: 10 to 12 servings.

## BLEU CHEESE MOLD

This blend of cheeses is a perfect foil for fresh fruits or vegetables.

2 3-oz. pkgs. cream cheese, softened
1 4-oz. pkg. bleu cheese
1 t. Worcestershire sauce
2 T. snipped parsley
½ t. salt
½ t. paprika
1 envelope unflavored gelatin
2 T. water
½ c. hot water
1 c. heavy cream, whipped

Mix the two cheeses until well blended. Add Worcestershire sauce, parsley, salt and paprika. Soften gelatin in cold water. Add hot water and stir until gelatin dissolves. Blend in cheese mixture and chill until mixture is of jelly-like consistency. Fold in whipped cream and pour into a lightly oiled 6-cup mold. Chill until firm. Makes 10 to 12 servings.

## RASPBERRY RING

A rhapsody in raspberry! Delicious with chicken or tuna salad.

2 10-oz. pkgs. frozen raspberries, thawed
  (save juice)
2 3-oz. pkgs. raspberry gelatin
3½ c. liquid (berry juice plus water)
1 c. sour cream
2 ripe bananas, sliced

Drain berries. Add water to juice to make 3½ cups liquid. Heat 2 cups of liquid to boiling, add gelatin and dissolve. Add remaining liquid and chill until of jelly-like consistency. Fold in drained berries, sour cream and sliced bananas. Pour into a lightly greased 6-cup mold. Chill until firm. Makes 10 to 12 servings.

# SALADS

## SALADE D'ÉPINARDS

This is the happiest way we know to eat spinach.

1 10-oz. bag fresh spinach
1 t. salt
½ t. pepper
2 t. Dijon mustard
2 T. red wine vinegar
½ c. olive oil
¼ t. lemon juice
5 radishes, sliced thin
1 small onion, sliced in rings

Wash spinach and dry completely. Break off stems and chill. Mix salt, pepper and mustard, then add vinegar. Beat in olive oil with fork until mixture has consistency of thin mayonnaise. Stir in lemon juice. Pour over chilled spinach, add sliced radishes and onions, toss. Yield: 4 to 6 servings.

---

Revive slightly wilted salad vegetables and greens in a bath of water and ice cubes.

---

## CHICKEN SALAD SUPREME

Dress up chicken salad with cantaloupe balls and serve in hollowed-out scalloped cantaloupe shells. Hollowed-out pineapple shells with the pineapple cubes added to the salad make attractive servers, too.

4 c. diced cooked chicken
½ c. celery, chopped
2 c. seedless grapes (optional)
½ t. salt
½ t. pepper
½ c. mayonnaise
½ c. sour cream
½ t. Dijon mustard
  Salted pecan halves or toasted almonds

Sprinkle chicken with 1 teaspoon olive oil or 1 tablespoon French dressing. Combine chicken, celery, grapes, salt and pepper and toss lightly with mayonnaise, sour cream and mustard. Add nuts. Serves 6 to 8.

## CAESAR SALAD

Get a man into the act. Encourage him to show off his culinary skills by tossing this salad at the table. Of course you will have all the ingredients ready. Great Caesar!

1 large head romaine lettuce, washed, dried and crisped
1 clove garlic
½ c. oil
1 c. ½-inch French bread cubes
¾ t. salt
¼ t. dry mustard
¼ t. freshly ground pepper
1½ t. Worcestershire sauce
6 anchovy fillets, drained and chopped
1 egg
2 T. grated parmesan cheese
2 T. lemon juice

Crush ½ clove of garlic and combine with oil in a covered jar. Let stand ½ hour. Heat 2 tablespoons of the oil-garlic mixture in a skillet. Trim crusts from bread and add bread cubes. Sauté until brown. Set aside. To remaining oil-garlic mixture, add lemon juice, salt, mustard, pepper, Worcestershire sauce and anchovies. Shake well. Bring 2 inches of water to a boil in a small pan. Turn off heat, place egg in water, let stand 1 minute, remove to cool. Whip into dressing.

Just before serving, rub inside of salad bowl with ½ clove of garlic; discard. Cut coarse ribs from romaine leaves and tear into bite-sized pieces in salad bowl. Shake dressing and pour over romaine. Sprinkle with cheese. Toss until well coated. Sprinkle bread cubes over salad, toss again and serve at once. Makes 4 to 6 servings.

## WATER CHESTNUT SALAD

Water chestnuts have practically no calories, so indulge yourself with the dressing.

½ c. mayonnaise
¼ c. sour half-and-half
1 T. tarragon vinegar
2 t. anchovy paste
⅛ c. chives, finely snipped
⅛ c. snipped parsley
½ clove garlic, minced
1 can water chestnuts, drained and sliced

Combine first 7 ingredients and pour over the water chestnuts. Chill several hours before serving. Makes 2 to 4 servings.

## SALADE NICOISE

You don't have to travel to sunny Spain for Salade Nicoise. Make it often and serve as an appetizer, a first course for dinner, or a summertime luncheon entrée.

      2  7½-oz. cans white tuna fish, drained
      1  qt. salad greens
         (or just enough to line platter)
     15  small ripe pitted olives
      6  hard-cooked eggs, cut in wedges
      4  tomatoes, quartered
      8 to 10 anchovy fillets
      2 to 4 T. wine vinegar
      1  small can sardines
      1  6-oz. jar marinated artichoke
         hearts, drained (save liquid)

One of two methods may be used in preparation:

1. Arrange all attractively on platter and sprinkle with a combination of vinegar and the artichoke marinade.

2. Toss tuna fish, greens, drained artichokes and olives in large bowl. Before serving, combine artichoke marinade and vinegar, pour over salad and toss gently. Place crossed strips of anchovies over all and arrange egg and tomato wedges along border. Omit sardines.

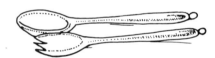

## CITRUS SALAD

Cool, colorful and refreshing.

      1  bunch romaine lettuce
      ½  lb. fresh spinach
      3  oranges, peeled and sectioned
      1 to 2 grapefruit, peeled and sectioned

Wash lettuce and spinach and break into bite-sized pieces. Combine fruits and greens in a salad bowl and toss gently with the following dressing.

### HONEY-LEMON DRESSING

      ½  c. sour cream
      ½  c. mayonnaise
     1½  T. lemon juice
      ¼  c. honey
      ½  t. dry mustard
         Celery salt to taste

Mix all ingredients together until well blended. Chill and serve. Serves 4 to 6.

## HALIBUT SALAD

Champagne tastes with a limited budget? Halibut Salad tastes very much like crabmeat.

      1  lb. halibut, thawed and drained
      1  carrot
      1  stalk celery
      1  onion, sliced
      1  t. salt

Cook halibut and vegetables in simmering salted water for 15 to 20 minutes. Do not boil. Fish will flake easily with a fork when done. Drain, cool and bone. Chill thoroughly. Flake the fish and dress with Sauce Louis. Garnish with sliced hard-cooked eggs and serve on lettuce. Makes 4 servings.

### SAUCE LOUIS

      1  c. mayonnaise
      1  t. horseradish
      1  t. Worcestershire sauce
      ½  t. salt
      ½  c. French dressing
      ¼  c. catsup or chili sauce

Mix all ingredients until well blended. Chill.

## CREAMY DRESSING (LOW-CAL)

      ½  c. buttermilk (or sour half-and-half)
      2  T. cottage cheese
      ¼  t. salt
      ¼  t. pepper
      2  snipped green onions
      ¼  t. dry mustard
      1  T. snipped parsley

Combine all ingredients in an electric blender and blend until smooth.

## MAYONNAISE DRESSING (LOW-CAL)

      ½  c. cottage cheese
      1  egg, beaten slightly
      ⅛  t. freshly ground pepper
      ⅛  t. dry mustard
      1  T. tarragon vinegar

Place all ingredients in an electric blender and blend at low speed until creamy.

Note: Change ratio of 2 parts oil to 1 part vinegar. By reversing, you can reduce calories in a 2 tablespoon serving from 160 to 80 calories. Season wine vinegar with minced onion, crushed garlic, dry mustard, salt, pepper, thyme or basil.

## SOUR CREAM DRESSING

| | |
|---|---|
| 1 c. sour cream | 1½ t. lemon juice |
| ¼ t. salt | ¼ c. honey |
| Celery salt to taste | ½ t. dry mustard |

Combine all ingredients and chill.

## FRENCH DRESSING NO. 1

| | |
|---|---|
| ¾ c. sugar (or sugar substitute) | 1 can tomato soup |
| | ½ c. salad oil |
| 1 t. dry mustard | 1 c. cider vinegar |
| 1 t. paprika | ½ c. green pepper, finely minced |
| 1 clove garlic | |
| 1 t. salt | |

Combine all ingredients. Beat until smooth with wire whisk or electric blender or mixer at top speed for 4 minutes. Refrigerate in jar until needed. Shake well before using.

## FRENCH DRESSING NO. 2

| | |
|---|---|
| ⅓ c. sugar | 1 t. paprika |
| 1 t. celery salt | ½ t. onion, minced (optional) |
| 1 c. oil | |
| 4 T. vinegar | 1 t. dry mustard |
| 1 t. salt | |

Combine all ingredients and blend until smooth. Chill.

## THOUSAND ISLAND DRESSING

1 c. mayonnaise
1 t. Worcestershire sauce
1 t. instant minced onion
¼ c. sweet pickle relish
2 t. green pepper, finely chopped
1 hard-cooked egg, finely chopped
1½ c. sour cream
½ c. chili sauce

Combine all ingredients, folding in sour cream last. Refrigerate.

## OIL AND VINEGAR

| | |
|---|---|
| 1 t. salt | 2 T. red wine vinegar |
| ½ t. pepper | ½ c. olive oil |
| 2 t. Dijon mustard | ¼ t. lemon juice |

Mix all ingredients, blend well. Chill.

# SALAD DRESSINGS

## CONDIMENTO DI ITALIANA

¼ c. olive oil
2 T. tarragon vinegar
½ t. sugar
½ t. dry mustard
Dash of pepper, freshly ground

Mix all ingredients together, blend well. Chill.

## VINAIGRETTE DRESSING

| | |
|---|---|
| 1 t. salt | 2 T. red wine vinegar |
| ½ t. pepper | ½ c. olive oil |
| 2 t. Dijon mustard | ½ t. lemon juice |

Mix all ingredients together, blend well. Chill.

## COLESLAW DRESSING

1 c. sour cream (or sour half-and-half)
½ c. mayonnaise
4 T. vinegar
2 t. sugar
Salt and pepper to taste
Celery salt to taste

Mix all ingredients and chill.

## ITALIAN SALAD DRESSING

½ c. olive oil
¼ c. wine vinegar
1 t. salt
1 small clove garlic, cut into small pieces
1½ T. sugar

Combine ingredients in a jar and shake well until thoroughly blended. Keep refrigerated. Shake well before using.

## GREEN GODDESS DRESSING

1 c. mayonnaise
½ c. sour cream
2 T. tarragon vinegar
1 clove garlic, minced
5 t. anchovy paste
¼ c. chives, snipped
¼ c. snipped parsley

Combine all ingredients. Refrigerate several hours before serving.

## HOT CHEESE BREAD

Your family will love the aroma of fresh bread baking, thanks to biscuit mix.

3¾ c. biscuit mix
1¼ c. shredded sharp cheddar cheese
2 T. poppy seed
1 egg, slightly beaten
1¼ c. milk

Mix together the cheese, biscuit mix and poppy seed. Stir in the egg and milk until blended. Then beat by hand for a minute or two. Sprinkle with a teaspoon of poppy seed. Bake in a greased loaf pan at 350° for 55 to 60 minutes. Cool for a few minutes before slicing.

## PUMPKIN BREAD

Pumpkin bread is nice to have on hand at holiday time, and it freezes well. It will keep 3 to 4 weeks in the refrigerator if wrapped tightly in foil.

| | |
|---|---|
| 3½ c. sifted flour | 4 eggs, beaten |
| 2 t. soda | ⅔ c. water |
| 1½ t. salt | 1 c. salad oil |
| 3 c. sugar | 2 c. canned |
| 1 t. nutmeg | pumpkin |
| 1 t. cinnamon | ¾ c. chopped nuts |

Sift together flour, soda, salt, sugar, nutmeg and cinnamon. Combine eggs, water, salad oil and pumpkin. Add to dry ingredients and mix only until well blended. Fold in nuts, pour batter into 2 well-greased loaf pans. Bake in a preheated 350° oven 1 hour or until a toothpick inserted into the center comes out clean.

## FRENCH OR ITALIAN BREAD

Everyone loves hot crusty French or Italian bread. Here are four different ways to serve it.

### GARLIC BREAD

½ c. (¼ lb.) butter or margarine, softened
1 large clove garlic, minced

Blend together.

### HERB BREAD

¼ lb. butter or margarine, softened
   Parsley, chives, thyme, tarragon, dill

Use two of the spices and combine with butter to taste.

### CHEESY-CHIVE BREAD

¼ lb. butter or margarine, softened
4 ozs. cheddar cheese, shredded
¼ c. snipped chives
2 T. yellow mustard

Blend all ingredients together.

### BOURBON STREET BREAD

½ c. snipped chives
½ c. grated parmesan cheese
¾ c. mayonnaise

Mix all ingredients together.

Cut bread with a sharp knife into 1-inch-thick slices and butter each slice on both sides with the spread of your choice. Reassemble loaf and wrap in aluminum foil. Bake in a pre-heated 375° oven 15 minutes. To brown and crisp loaf, open foil and bake 5 minutes longer at 400°.

## BATTER BREAD

Famous southern cooks say that good Batter Bread cannot possibly be made from a written recipe, but this is a very satisfactory try.

| | |
|---|---|
| 1½ c. water | 2 t. baking powder |
| ⅛ lb. butter | ½ t. salt |
| 1 c. white cornmeal | 2 c. buttermilk |
| | 2 to 3 T. oil |
| 3 eggs | |

Bring water to a boil, add butter and melt. Remove from heat and add cornmeal. Stir well. Add eggs, one at a time, stirring well. Then add baking powder, salt and buttermilk. Stir until smooth and pour into a heated and well-greased (using the oil) 8- to 9-inch pan. Bake at 400° for 35 to 40 minutes. Makes 4 to 6 servings.

## CRANBERRY NUT BREAD

Nut breads are a happy holiday thought. They will taste even better and be easier to slice if they are tightly wrapped and set aside for a day.

  2 c. flour
  1 c. sugar
1½ t. baking powder
  ½ t. soda
  1 t. salt
  ¾ c. orange juice
  1 T. grated orange rind
  1 egg, well beaten
  ¼ c. butter or margarine, melted
  2 c. cranberries, coarsely chopped
     or halved
  ½ c. chopped nuts

Sift together flour, sugar, baking powder, soda and salt. Combine orange juice, rind, egg and melted butter or margarine. Add to dry ingredients and mix only until flour mixture is moistened. Carefully fold in cranberries and chopped nuts. Spoon into 2 greased loaf pans and bake in a 350° oven 1 hour.

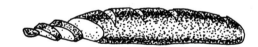

## COLD OVEN POPOVERS

A quick version of the classic popover that dramatically shortens the usual preparation time of the original.

| | |
|---|---|
| 3 eggs | 1 c. flour |
| 1 c. milk | ½ t. salt |

Butter 6 custard cups heavily. Beat eggs, milk, flour and salt until smooth. Pour batter into cups, place in a cold oven, turn oven to 450° and bake for 30 minutes. Pierce with a toothpick to hold for a while without collapsing.

> Use waxed paper to grease molds and pans.

## FRENCH TOAST SANDWICH

Create a hearty brunch treat using your favorite sandwich combination of meats and cheese. Serve with a tossed salad or a fresh fruit bowl. A French Toast Sandwich makes a delicious luncheon.

    4 slices white bread
      Chicken, turkey, ham, luncheon meat, sliced
      American, cheddar, Swiss, Gruyère cheese, sliced
    1 egg
    ¼ c. milk

Beat egg lightly, add milk, stir. Dip the sandwiches, filled with meat and cheese, into the mixture, turning to coat both sides. Sauté in butter on both sides, using a skillet or electric frying pan, until golden brown. Serve with mustard or pancake syrup. Makes 2 sandwiches.

## LAYERED CHEESE SOUFFLÉ

Even the most well-run households occasionally have some slightly stale bread, and that's just what is needed for this fluffy never-fail soufflé. It is a joy for breakfast, luncheon or dinner.

    10 slices slightly stale white bread
     6 eggs, beaten
     2 c. milk
    ¾ t. salt
     1 t. dry mustard
     1 t. Worcestershire sauce
     2 c. sharp cheddar cheese, grated
       Tuna, shrimp, crabmeat, or turkey slices (optional)
     3 T. butter

Trim crusts off bread. Combine eggs, milk, salt, mustard and Worcestershire sauce, beating well. Grease an 11 x 13-inch pan and alternate layers of bread and cheese, ending with bread. If seafood or poultry is used add it to the cheese layer. Cover with the liquid mixture and refrigerate for 3 to 4 hours or overnight.

Bring to room temperature, dot with butter and bake in a preheated 350° oven 1 hour. Makes 4 to 6 servings.

Grilled ham or bacon go well with this soufflé.

## FRENCH BAKED PANCAKE

Happiness is Sunday morning brunch; this cheese-filled pancake will bake while you prepare the rest of your brunch.

    ¼ lb. butter or          1¼ c. milk
      margarine               2 c. flour
    4 t. sugar               1½ t. baking powder
    3 large eggs

Cream butter and sugar, add eggs. Add flour and baking powder alternately with milk and mix well. Place half of the batter (about 1½ cups) into a well-greased 13 x 9-inch baking dish.

### FILLING

    1½ lbs. creamed          1 t. salt
      cottage cheese          2 eggs
    3 T. melted butter

Beat together cottage cheese, butter, salt and eggs. Spoon filling over batter and top with remaining batter. Bake in a 350° oven 45 minutes until golden brown. Cut into squares and serve hot with sour cream, preserves, honey or pancake syrup. Serves 6 to 8.

> To soften butter or margarine for creaming, cut thin slices into bowl.

## BUTTERMILK BISCUITS

Very Southern and traditionally served with Virginia ham, these melt-in-the-mouth biscuits are good buttered and served with any meat or jam.

    1¾ c. sifted flour       ½ t. soda
     1 t. salt               ¼ c. shortening
     2 t. baking powder      ⅔ c. buttermilk
     1 t. sugar

Cut shortening into dry ingredients until the consistency of cornmeal. Make a well, add buttermilk. Stir until dough leaves side of bowl, about ½ minute. Turn dough onto floured board and knead lightly for ½ minute. Pat with floured hand to ¼- to ½-inch thick. Cut with floured biscuit cutter. Bake at 450° for 10 to 12 minutes. Makes 10 to 12 biscuits.

## BLINTZES

Take the time, then take the credit for this versatile filled pancake, delicious as a brunch or luncheon entrée or as a dinner dessert.

### PANCAKE

| | |
|---|---|
| 3 eggs | 1 c. flour |
| 1⅓ c. water | ¼ t. salt |

Beat eggs, add half of the water, the flour, the salt, and the remaining water. Beat until smooth in blender, with electric mixer or with whip. Let rest while mixing the filling.

### FILLING

1 lb. dry cottage cheese
2 eggs
½ t. vanilla
1 t. sugar (optional)
½ t. cinnamon (optional)

Combine cheese, eggs and seasonings and beat until smooth. Lightly grease a 6-, 7-, or 8-inch skillet and heat on top of stove. Pour just enough batter in pan to coat thinly, tilting it from side to side and pouring out excess. Fry only on one side and turn out, brown side up, on a towel. Repeat until batter is used up, adding a little more water if it thickens. Place 1 heaping teaspoon of filling on each pancake and fold envelope-style. Refrigerate or freeze until ready to fry or bake. Sauté in butter or oil until brown on both sides or bake in a buttered pan in a 375° oven for 35 minutes or until brown. Serve with sour cream and hot blueberry, cherry or strawberry sauce or preserves. Or serve with sour cream and caviar and omit sugar and cinnamon.

Note: If frozen, thaw in refrigerator before browning. Makes 22 to 24 blintzes.

### BLUEBERRY SAUCE

1 can blueberries, drained (save juice)
1 T. cornstarch
2 T. sugar
1 T. lemon juice

Blend cornstarch and sugar. Stir into blueberry juice and cook over low heat until clear. Add lemon juice and berries and heat.

> Have egg whites at room temperature before beating. They will double in volume.

## ESTHER'S CHEESE DREAMS

To stretch the food budget and win acclaim, try Cheese Dreams for brunch, luncheon or a meatless supper.

| | |
|---|---|
| ¼ c. butter | ¼ t. salt |
| ¼ c. shortening | ¼ t. baking powder |
| 1¼ c. flour | ½ c. sour cream |

Mix pastry ingredients as for pie dough. Divide into 4 parts. Wrap in waxed paper and chill ½ to 1 hour. Roll out on floured waxed paper. Put cheese filling on dough and roll like a jelly roll. Cut into 2-inch slices, dot each with butter, and bake on a greased cookie sheet in a preheated 350° oven 40 minutes or until golden brown. Serve hot with sour cream and blueberry sauce or frozen strawberries.

### FILLING

1¼ lbs. dry cottage cheese
2 eggs
2 t. melted butter
¼ t. salt

Mix all together until well blended.

Note: Cheese Dreams may be frozen unbaked.

## GRANOLA

Close the nutrition gap with this delicious and nutritious toasty cereal. Serve with cold milk or use as an ice cream or pudding topping.

3 c. old-fashioned oats, uncooked
½ c. wheat germ
1 c. flaked or shredded coconut
½ c. chopped nuts
½ c. sesame seeds
½ t. salt
¼ c. honey
¼ c. oil
½ t. vanilla
1 c. raisins

In a large bowl combine all ingredients except the raisins. Mix together thoroughly.

Bake mixture on a large baking sheet in a preheated 325° oven for about 20 minutes until golden brown. Shake pan occasionally. Add raisins. Cool and stir with fork until crumbly. Store in covered refrigerator jar.

## CHERRIES JUBILEE

Dim the lights and flame this delicious and dramatic dessert at the table.

1 1-lb. can pitted Bing cherries, drained
¾ c. currant jelly
½ c. Kirsch (or brandy)
Ice cream balls

In a chafing dish over direct heat, melt currant jelly, stirring gently. When jelly has melted, add cherries. Heat slowly until simmering. Pour Kirsch into center of fruit. Do not stir or it will not flame. Let it heat, then light carefully with a match. Immediately spoon flaming cherries over ice cream. Makes 4 to 6 servings.

## CRANBERRY PUDDING

This very special recipe is unique to the Midwest, and has become a tradition in many households at holiday time. It is simple to prepare.

    1 egg, slightly beaten
    1 heaping T. sugar
    ½ c. light molasses
    ⅓ c. hot water
    1½ c. flour
    2 t. baking soda
    ½ t. salt
    2 c. fresh cranberries, washed and drained

Combine all ingredients in order listed. Pour into a greased mold and steam for 1 hour over simmering water, tightly covered. Make a steamer by punching holes in an aluminum pie pan and inverting it in the bottom of a saucepan with a tight-fitting cover. Serve warm with the following sauce. No other sauce will do!

### SAUCE

| | |
|---|---|
| 1 c. coffee cream | ¼ t. salt |
| ¼ lb. butter | 1 t. vanilla |
| 1 c. sugar | |

Heat cream, butter, sugar and salt to the boiling point. Remove from heat and add vanilla. Serve warm over warm pudding. Use the sauce liberally, as the pudding is tart.

## LEMON SURPRISE

A lemon sponge with custard sauce underneath is really a surprise.

    4 eggs, separated
    1½ c. milk
    1 c. sugar
    2 T. flour
    ¼ t. salt
    1 lemon, juice and grated rind

Beat egg yolks with milk. Mix together flour, sugar and salt and add to egg and milk mixture. Add lemon juice and rind. Beat egg whites until stiff and fold into custard. Pour into custard cups, then set in a shallow pan with water halfway up the cups. Bake in a preheated 350° oven 30 minutes. Refrigerate. Top with whipped cream and a cherry if desired. Serves 6.

## CHOCOLATE CUPS

One, two, three chocolate crinkle cups can be made days in advance and carefully stored in the refrigerator.

8 squares semisweet chocolate
8 to 10 cupcake liners

Melt chocolate in the top of a double boiler over hot, not boiling, water. With a small spoon or pastry brush coat the insides of the paper cups with a thin layer of chocolate. Place cups in a muffin pan and refrigerate until firm.

Carefully peel paper from cups and refrigerate until ready to serve. Or fill cups with ice cream and place in the freezer.

Cups also may be filled with coffee ice cream or Crème Café and topped with whipped cream, chocolate curls or nuts. Makes 8 to 10 cups.

## CRÈME CAFÉ

A dessert spectacular; for a super spectacle, spoon into Chocolate Cups and top with whipped cream. Serve in champagne glasses if desired.

    1 c. coffee
    ½ lb. marshmallows
    2 T. brandy
    ½ pt. whipping cream, whipped
      (or whipped topping)

Melt marshmallows in coffee in a double boiler over hot water. Cool, add brandy. Fold in chilled whipped cream. Garnish with pecan or walnut half or a dollop of whipped cream if desired. Serves 6.

# CHOCOLATE MOUSSE

Sophisticated Chocolate Mousse in two versions. If you are cholesterol-conscious, try No. 2.

### CHOCOLATE MOUSSE NO. 1

½ lb. German sweet cooking chocolate
5 eggs, separated
1 c. heavy cream, whipped
1 T. Grand Marnier (or Triple-Sec)
3 T. strong coffee

Melt chocolate in a double boiler over hot, not boiling, water. Cool. Beat egg yolks until thick and lemon-colored. Add liqueur and coffee. Combine with chocolate and blend until smooth. Beat egg whites until stiff. Fold carefully into chocolate mixture. Fold whipped cream into mixture and pour or spoon into glasses or greased mold. Makes 8 to 10 servings.

### CHOCOLATE MOUSSE NO. 2

2 egg yolks
1 12-oz. pkg. semisweet chocolate pieces
1 c. scalded milk
½ t. instant coffee crystals
3 ozs. brandy
4 egg whites
½ c. sugar
Whipped cream

Put egg yolks, chocolate, scalded milk, coffee and brandy in blender. Blend on high speed until chocolate chips liquefy. In a separate bowl, beat egg whites, slowly adding sugar and beating until very firm. Fold into chocolate mixture. Do not stir or beat. Refrigerate 2 hours. Serve with a dollop of whipped cream. Makes 12 4-oz. servings.

# FRAISES BRÛLÉE
## (Strawberries and Cream)

Simplicity is sophistication. Here is a festive dessert with a French accent.

1 qt. fresh strawberries, washed and hulled
1 pt. heavy cream, whipped
1 c. brown sugar
1 T. Kirsch
3 T. brandy

Cover the bottom of a 2-quart casserole or soufflé dish with berries. Add enough Kirsch and brandy to just cover the fruit. Add 2 inches of whipped cream and a 1-inch layer of brown sugar. Refrigerate 4 hours. To serve, place under broiler to brown lightly and quickly for 1 to 1½ minutes. Makes 8 servings.

# MACAROON MOUSSE

Cool, shimmering, amber elegance for a grand finale.

1 pkg. macaroon cookies
½ c. bourbon
½ c. water
1½ T. unflavored gelatin
4 eggs, separated
2 c. milk
1 c. sugar
½ pt. whipping cream, whipped

Soak macaroons in bourbon until most of liquid is absorbed. Line a lightly greased melon-shaped 4-cup mold with macaroons. Add gelatin to water and let stand 10 minutes. Beat egg yolks in a large saucepan. Add gelatin, milk, sugar and stir well. Cook over low heat until the mixture comes to a rolling boil, stirring constantly. Remove from heat. Beat egg whites until stiff. Fold them into the hot mixture, which will not be smooth. Pour into lined mold. Refrigerate overnight. Unmold and decorate with whipped cream around the white sides, leaving the amber gelatin top clear. Makes 12 servings.

# FRAISES ET FRAMBOISES
## (Strawberries and Raspberries)

Use your prettiest crystal sherbets, parfaits, or champagne glasses so that the brilliant color of the two fruits will whet your appetite for the taste to follow.

1 to 1½ qts. strawberries, washed and hulled
½ c. sugar
1 10-oz. pkg. frozen raspberries, thawed
¼ c. Cointreau (or Triple-Sec)
2 T. powdered sugar
1 t. lemon juice

Refrigerate the strawberries, sprinkled with sugar, for 2 hours. Just before serving place raspberries, powdered sugar, lemon juice and Cointreau in blender and blend for about 1 minute or until smooth. Pour over individual servings of chilled strawberries. Garnish with a fresh mint leaf. Makes 6 to 8 servings.

## FLAN

The simplicity of this recipe should not mislead you. It is a 1, 2, 3 way of preparing the classic dessert of Spain.

1 can sweetened    3 eggs
   condensed milk    Brown sugar
2 c. whole milk

Beat eggs in a bowl, add sweetened condensed milk and whole milk and beat well. Pour mixture into individual custard cups. Place in a pan of water that comes up two-thirds of the way to sides of cup. Bake in a preheated 350° oven 1 hour or until a knife inserted in the center comes out clean. Remove from water bath and cool. Spread 1 tablespoon of brown sugar on top of each flan, spreading lightly to cover. Set under broiler for a couple of minutes until bubbly, watching carefully. Remove from oven and refrigerate. Makes 6 to 8 flans.

## HOT FUDGE SAUCE

Fabulous! Pass it hot at the table.

3 ozs. baking chocolate
1 T. butter
1 c. sugar
1 small can evaporated milk
½ t. vanilla

Melt chocolate and butter together in a heavy saucepan. Stir in sugar and milk. Continue stirring until sauce is thick. Add vanilla. Reheat over hot water if desired.

## TORTONI

To complete an Italian dinner try this unusual dessert.

1 8-oz. pkg. cream cheese, softened
1 c. white corn syrup
1 c. milk
1 c. broken macaroons
½ c. chopped pecans
1 t. vanilla flavoring
1 t. almond extract
   Maraschino cherries

Mix cream cheese, syrup and milk until smooth. Stir in remaining ingredients. Spoon into paper baking cups set in muffin pan. Freeze until firm. Serve partially frozen and garnished with half a maraschino cherry. Makes 4 cups. Serves 16.

## GEORGIAN TRIFLE

This dessert was originally created as a way to use stale cake. Our short cut to the custard sauce will send you hurrying to the market to buy fresh sponge cake.

1 sponge cake (or packaged shortcake shells)
1 jar raspberry jam
½ c. sherry
1 pkg. French vanilla instant pudding
2 c. milk
½ pt. whipping cream, whipped
   Strawberries, raspberries (optional)
   Slivered almonds (optional)

Split sponge cake into 1½-inch layers and spread each half with raspberry jam. Put cake together again and cut into cubes. Place in a crystal bowl and dampen with ¼ cup of the sherry, enough to flavor the cake but not to make it soggy.

Prepare pudding mix according to package directions and fold in remaining sherry. Whip cream and fold a quarter of it into the custard. Pour custard over cake cubes. Heap remaining whipped cream on top. Garnish with berries or slivered almonds. Refrigerate several hours before serving. Makes 8 to 10 servings.

## CHOCOLATE MOUSSE PIE

Delicious chocolate! Served on a pretty plate, this chocolate pie is a heavenly treat.

1 9-inch baked pastry or crumb shell
⅔ c. sugar
¼ c. cocoa
⅛ t. salt
1 c. milk
1 envelope unflavored gelatin
¼ c. cold water
½ t. vanilla
1 c. heavy cream, whipped

Combine sugar, cocoa and salt in a saucepan. Stir in milk and heat to boiling. Remove from heat. Dissolve gelatin in cold water and stir into hot mixture. Chill until mixture begins to thicken. Add vanilla. Fold in whipped cream and pour into pie shell. Chill until firm. Garnish with additional whipped cream if desired.

# TORTES

### ELSIE'S SCHAUM TORTE

A gourmet dessert that's prepared in minutes and raved about for hours.

|  |  |
|---|---|
| 9 egg whites | ½ t. salt |
| 2¾ c. sugar | ½ pt. whipping |
| 1 T. vinegar | cream, whipped |
| ½ t. cream of tartar | Strawberries |
| 1 t. almond extract | |

Preheat oven to 400°. Put first 6 ingredients into a large mixing bowl and beat until meringue holds its shape. Then beat some more, and still some more. Spoon into a 9-inch springform with an aluminum foil collar. Turn oven down to 275° and bake torte 1½ hours. Keep in oven until cool. Frost with whipped cream, refrigerate and garnish with fresh strawberries before serving. Serves 10 to 12.

Note: Do not bake on rainy or humid days.

### APRICOT TORTE

A sweet show-off that's easy to make.

½ lb. vanilla wafers, crushed
1 c. butter
1⅓ c. confectioners' sugar
3 eggs
1 large can peeled apricots, drained
1 c. pecans, chopped
1 pt. whipping cream, whipped

Line an 8 x 12-inch pan with waxed paper. Crush vanilla wafers into fine crumbs. Cream together butter, sugar and eggs until smooth. Cut up the apricots. Arrange in layers in the following order: crumbs (reserve 3 tablespoons crumbs for top), butter mixture, apricots, nuts, whipped cream, sprinkle of crumbs. Refrigerate for 12 hours. Makes 12 servings.

## QUICK TORTES

Two desserts-for-a-crowd that must be made ahead and refrigerated overnight. One is lemony, one is chocolaty; both are spectacular, with a checkerboard design visible when sliced.

### LEMON TORTE

1 large or 1½ small angel food cakes
1 T. unflavored gelatin
¼ c. cold water
6 egg yolks
⅔ c. lemon juice
2 t. grated lemon rind
¾ c. sugar
¾ c. sugar
6 egg whites
1 pt. whipping cream, whipped
Shredded coconut (optional)

Trim brown crusts from cake and cut cake into cubes. Soften gelatin in the cold water. Combine egg yolks, ¾ cup sugar, lemon juice and rind. Cook over hot (not boiling) water. Stir until mixture coats spoon. Remove from heat and add gelatin, stirring until dissolved. Cook until partially thickened. Beat egg whites, gradually adding ¾ cup sugar. Beat until stiff. Fold into custard and mix with cake cubes. Pour into a lightly oiled torte pan or large bowl and refrigerate overnight. Remove from pan and frost with whipped cream. Sprinkle with coconut if desired. Serves 12.

### CHOCOLATE TORTE

1 large angel food cake
1 c. sugar
1½ pkgs. unflavored gelatin
¼ c. cold water
¾ c. boiling water
5 eggs, separated
2 squares baking chocolate
1 pt. whipping cream, whipped

Trim brown crust from cake and cut cake into cubes. Melt chocolate and cool. Dissolve gelatin in the cold water. Add boiling water and let stand. Beat egg yolks; add sugar, chocolate and gelatin. In a separate bowl, beat egg whites until stiff but not dry. Fold into chocolate mixture. Fold in cake cubes and pour into a lightly oiled springform or large bowl. Refrigerate at least 8 hours. Unmold and frost with whipped cream and shaved chocolate. Serves 12.

## STRAWBERRY BAVARIAN SPONGE TORTE

2 pkgs. strawberry gelatin
1 c. boiling water
2 pkgs. frozen sliced strawberries, slightly thawed
½ pt. whipping cream, whipped (or whipped topping)
1 sponge cake, cut in cubes
Whipped cream to decorate
Fresh berries to decorate

Dissolve gelatin in boiling water. Add berries and allow to partially thicken. Fold in ½ pint whipped cream. Toss with cake cubes and place in a greased springform or large mixing bowl. Chill torte overnight. Turn out on platter and frost with whipped cream. Garnish with whole strawberries. Serves 10 to 12.

 # CAKES

## CHOCOLATE CHERRY CAKE

Rich and chocolaty! Indulge yourself.

      1  c. sugar
    ¼  lb. butter
      2  eggs
      2  squares baking chocolate, melted and
          cooled
      1  T. cocoa
      1  t. baking soda
      1  c. sour cream
    16  maraschino cherries, quartered
    ¼  c. maraschino cherry juice
  1⅓  c. sifted cake flour
    ⅛  t. salt

Cream sugar and butter together. Beat in
eggs, one at a time. Add chocolate and cocoa.
In a separate bowl stir baking soda into sour
cream, stirring until it makes a clicking sound.
Add with the cherries to the mixture. Add salt
to flour. Beat in flour alternately with the
cherry juice. Place in a well-greased 9 x
12-inch baking pan and bake in a preheated
350° oven 35 minutes. Frost with Chocolate
Glaze (see frostings).

## BOURBON POUND CAKE

Your husband will be glad to donate a little of
his good bourbon to this cause.

    ½  lb. butter
  1½  c. sugar
      4  eggs, separated
  1½  c. sifted flour
      1  t. vanilla extract
      1  t. almond extract
    ¼  c. (scant) bourbon
    ½  c. pecan halves

Cream butter and 1 cup of the sugar until light
and fluffy. Add egg yolks one at a time, beating well after each addition. Add flour alternately with flavorings and bourbon, beating
smooth after each addition. Beat egg whites
until stiff but not dry. Beat remaining ½ cup of
sugar gradually into egg whites. Fold batter
gently into meringue. Sprinkle nuts into bottom of well-greased 9-inch tube or bundt pan
and carefully turn batter into pan. Bake at 350°
for 60 to 70 minutes or until a tester inserted in
center comes out clean. Cool. Invert pan to
turn out cake.

## FRUIT KUCHEN

An old-fashioned German dessert.

| | |
|---|---|
| 1¼ c. flour | 1 egg, slightly |
| 1 t. baking powder | beaten |
| 1 T. sugar | 1 T. milk |
| ¼ lb. butter | |

Mix first 3 ingredients together, then add
butter and mix or cut in as for piecrust. Mix
together egg and milk and add to above. Press
in sides and bottom of 9 x 13-inch pan.

### FILLING

    4 to 6 peaches, peeled and halved
      1  egg, slightly beaten
      1  c. sour cream
  1½  T. flour
    ¾  c. sugar

Place peaches on crust, cut side up. Mix egg,
sour cream, flour and sugar. Pour over fruit.

### STREUSEL

| | |
|---|---|
| ¾ c. sugar | 2 T. flour |
| 2 T. butter | ½ t. cinnamon |

Cream sugar and butter; cut in flour and
cinnamon.

Cover fruit with streusel and bake at 350° for
45 minutes or until fruit is baked and streusel
is a delicate brown.

Note: Use 1½ cups cherry or blueberry pie
filling instead of peaches if desired. Pitted
plums or peeled quartered apples are also
good.

## HOT MILK CAKE

This cake, with its down-home taste, needs
no frosting.

| | |
|---|---|
| 5 eggs, well beaten | 1 c. milk |
| 2 c. sugar | 1 t. baking powder |
| 2½ c. flour | 1 t. vanilla |
| ¼ c. butter | 1 t. lemon extract |

Add sugar to the beaten eggs and beat. Add
flour a little at a time. Add baking powder
with the last of the flour. Heat milk and butter
to boiling point and pour it over the first mixture. Stir in well. Add flavorings. Bake in a
preheated 325° oven in an ungreased tube pan
for 40 to 50 minutes.

## COFFEE CAKE SUPREME

Nostalgic for coffee cake the way Mother used to make it? Try this.

½ lb. butter or margarine
1 c. sugar
3 eggs
3 c. sifted flour
2½ t. baking powder
½ t. salt
8 ozs. sour cream (or sour cream substitute)
½ t. baking soda
1 t. vanilla

Cream butter and sugar. Add eggs and beat until light and fluffy. Sift flour, baking powder and salt several times. Combine baking soda and sour cream. Add alternately with flour, ending with flour. Add vanilla.

### STREUSEL

¾ c. brown sugar
½ t. cinnamon
¾ c. chopped nuts

Grease a bundt pan well and dust with flour. Mix streusel ingredients together and sprinkle pan with a third of the mixture, then a third of cake batter, repeating layers in thirds. Bake in 350° oven 1 hour. Invert pan onto cookie or cake rack to cool.

## SUMMER FRUITCAKE

The surprise ingredient in this cake is watermelon pickles, available year-round. And this cake takes only a few minutes to prepare.

1 c. sifted flour
¾ c. sugar
1 t. baking powder
½ t. salt
3 c. pecan halves
1 t. vanilla extract
1½ c. drained, cut-up watermelon pickles
1 c. maraschino cherries, drained and halved
3 eggs

Grease bottoms and sides of two 8½ x 4½ x 2½-inch loaf pans. Mix and sift flour, sugar, baking powder and salt; add nuts, pickles and cherries and mix. Beat eggs slightly; add extract. Add to flour mixture and mix until ingredients are well combined. Bake in a preheated 300° oven 1 hour. Makes two 1¼-pound cakes.

## ORANGE BRUNCH CAKE

Cheerful and sunny for coffee time or Sunday brunch.

1 6-oz. can (¾ c.) frozen orange juice concentrate
2 c. sifted flour
1 c. sugar
1 t. soda
1 t. salt
¼ lb. butter or margarine
½ c. milk
2 eggs
1 c. raisins
⅓ c. chopped nuts

Grease and flour bottom of a 13 x 9-inch pan. In a large mixer bowl, combine ½ cup orange juice concentrate with flour, sugar, soda, salt, butter, milk and eggs. Blend at lowest speed of mixer 30 seconds. Beat 3 minutes at medium speed. Fold in raisins and nuts. Pour into pan. Bake in preheated 350° oven 30 to 40 minutes. Drizzle remaining orange juice concentrate over warm cake. Sprinkle with topping.

### TOPPING

⅓ c. sugar
¼ c. chopped nuts
1 t. cinnamon

Combine all ingredients in a small bowl.

# GREEK HONEY CAKE

Moist, rich and sweet, this is a traditional Greek dessert.

- ¾ c. butter
- ¾ c. sugar
- 3 eggs
- 1 c. flour, sifted
- 1½ t. baking powder
- ½ t. salt
- ½ t. cinnamon
- ¼ c. milk
- ½ t. grated orange rind
- 1 c. chopped walnuts

Cream butter and sugar well. Add eggs, one at a time, beating well after each addition. Sift together flour, baking powder, salt and cinnamon and add to batter. Stir in milk and orange rind. Beat well and stir in nuts. Pour into a greased and floured 9 x 9-inch pan. Bake in a preheated 350° oven 30 minutes or until done. Remove from oven, cut into diamond shapes in pan while still hot. Pour cold syrup over the cake and refrigerate for at least 1 to 2 hours before serving.

### SYRUP

- ½ c. sugar
- 1 c. honey
- ¾ c. water
- 1 t. lemon juice

Mix sugar, honey and water in a saucepan. Simmer 5 minutes. Skim, add lemon juice, boil 2 minutes and cool.

# BLUEBERRY CAKE

Quick, easy, economical and freezes like a dream. A winner for a church or school bake sale!

- ¼ lb. butter or margarine
- ¾ c. sugar
- 1 egg
- ½ c. milk
- 1 t. vanilla
- 2 c. flour
- 2 t. baking powder
- ½ t. salt
- 1 pt. blueberries

Cream butter or margarine until soft. Beat in sugar and add egg. Beat until fluffy. Stir in milk and vanilla until blended. Stir in flour, salt and baking powder. Fold in blueberries. Spoon into a greased 9 x 9-inch cake pan.

### TOPPING

- ½ c. sugar
- ⅛ stick butter or margarine
- ½ t. cinnamon

Mix all ingredients together lightly with a fork until crumbly. Spread on top of cake batter. Bake at 350° for 50 minutes.

# DANISH PUFF

Come over for coffee. A special treat, Scandinavian-style.

### BOTTOM LAYER

- 1 c. sifted flour
- ¼ lb. butter
- 2 T. water

Preheat oven to 350°. Measure flour into bowl. Cut in butter. Sprinkle with the water and mix with a fork. Round into a ball and divide in half. Pat dough with hands into two 12 x 3-inch strips. Place strips 3 inches apart on ungreased baking sheet.

### TOP LAYER

- ¼ lb. butter
- 1 c. water
- 1 t. almond extract
- 1 c. sifted flour
- 3 eggs

Mix butter and water in a saucepan and bring to a rolling boil. Add almond extract and remove from heat. Stir in flour immediately, beating vigorously with a wooden spoon. When smooth and thick add one egg at a time, beating again after each addition until smooth. Divide in half and spread one half evenly over each strip of pastry. Bake about 60 minutes, until topping is crisp and nicely browned. Frost with a powdered sugar icing and sprinkle generously with chopped nuts.

### POWDERED SUGAR ICING

- 1½ c. powdered sugar
- 2 T. boiling water
- 1 t. lemon juice

Mix together and blend until smooth.

## ABBREVIATIONS

- t. — teaspoon
- T. — tablespoon
- c. — cup
- pkg. — package
- pt. — pint
- qt. — quart
- oz. — ounce
- lb. — pound

# CHOCOLATE CAKE

Choc-o-holics will particularly enjoy this dessert. It is economical, both cost- and time-wise.

| | |
|---|---|
| 3 T. butter | 2 t. baking powder |
| 1½ squares baking chocolate | ¼ t. salt |
| | ½ c. milk |
| 1 c. sugar | 2 eggs |
| 1 c. flour | 1 t. vanilla |

Preheat oven to 350°. Put chocolate and butter in a baking dish and place in the oven to melt. In a large electric mixer bowl, measure and combine sugar, flour, baking powder and salt. Remove melted chocolate-butter mixture from oven and cool. Add cooled mixture to mixing bowl and beat at low speed of electric mixer for a couple of minutes. Add eggs, milk and vanilla and beat for 5 minutes at high speed. Turn into a greased 9 x 9-inch pan and bake 35 minutes at 350°. When cool either turn out of pan or frost in the pan with half of the recipe for Butter Cream Frosting Superb (see frostings).

# FROSTINGS

## CONFECTIONERS' ICING

  6 T. butter, softened
1½ c. powdered sugar
  1 T. milk
  1 t. vanilla

Cream butter and sugar together. Add a little milk, cream well, add more milk if too stiff. Add vanilla and mix well.

### VARIATIONS

Omit milk and add 1 tablespoon orange juice and ½ teaspoon grated orange rind, or 1 tablespoon lemon juice and ½ teaspoon grated lemon rind.

## BUTTER CREAM FROSTING SUPERB

  1 c. milk
  4 T. flour
  2 T. coffee or 2 squares baking chocolate, melted (optional)
½ lb. butter
    (or ¼ lb. butter and ¼ lb. margarine)
  1 c. sugar
  1 t. vanilla

Mix milk, coffee or chocolate and flour together. Bring to a boil, lower heat and simmer until thick and smooth. Cool to room temperature, placing a small pat of butter on top. Beat butter and sugar together until light and fluffy. Add cooled flour mixture and beat at low speed of electric mixer 2 to 3 minutes. Add vanilla and blend. Sprinkle jimmies, nuts or coconut over the top if desired.

## CHOCOLATE GLAZE

An easy frosting for brownies or cake.

  1 1-oz. square unsweetened chocolate
  2 T. water
¼ c. butter
  1 c. powdered sugar
  1 t. vanilla

Combine chocolate, water and butter in a saucepan. Stir over low heat until chocolate and butter are melted. Remove from heat. Add sugar, blend well. Stir in vanilla.

## WHIPPED CREAM FROSTING

  1 t. unflavored gelatin
  4 T. cold water
  1 c. whipping cream (or frozen whipped topping)
¼ c. powdered sugar
¼ t. vanilla

Combine gelatin and cold water. Dissolve over hot water and let stand. Beat whipping cream slightly. Pour cooled gelatin into cream. Add sugar gradually, then vanilla. Beat until stiff. Chill in refrigerator 10 minutes before frosting cake. Cake may be frosted hours before serving and returned to refrigerator. Add one of the variations if desired.

### VARIATIONS

¼ c. chocolate syrup
½ c. crushed pineapple, drained
    Sweetened cocoa mix to taste

Sprinkle top with one of the following:

Toasted coconut
Chopped nuts
Grated or shaved sweet or semisweet
    chocolate
Crushed toffee bars
Whole strawberries

Plain, sweetened or flavored whipped cream frosts a cake, too, but holds only a short time.

## BROILED TOPPING

The finishing touch for a cake mix or a plain bakery cake.

⅓ c. butter, melted
⅔ c. brown sugar
¼ c. cream or evaporated milk
½ c. coconut
½ c. chopped pecans

Mix all ingredients together and spread on a baked 8- or 9-inch cake. Broil carefully at low heat until bubbly and toasted. Watch it carefully to prevent burning.

## BASIC CHEESE PIE

A dessert that always gets a smile; say, "cheese pie."

 1  9-inch unbaked pie shell
    or graham cracker crust
 1  8-oz. pkg. cream cheese, softened
 ½  c. sugar
 3  eggs
 2  T. flour
 ⅓  c. milk
 1  t. vanilla

Put cream cheese in a bowl and beat until soft and smooth. Add sugar gradually and continue beating until smooth. Stir in flour and unbeaten eggs and beat. Add milk and vanilla and beat until cheese disappears. The filling will be liquid.

Pour filling into unbaked pie shell and bake at 350° for 40 minutes or until firm and delicately brown. To test doneness, insert tip of table knife into center of pie. If it comes out clean, pie is done.

### TOPPING

 1  c. sour cream
 2  T. sugar
 ½  t. vanilla

Combine sour cream, sugar and vanilla. Spread on top of pie and return to oven for 10 minutes.

If preferred, omit topping and spread a fruit glaze on cool pie. Chill again before serving.

## FRESH STRAWBERRY PIE

Pretty as a picture, this pie is fabulous.

 1  9-inch graham cracker crust or
    baked pie shell
 2  pts. strawberries, washed and hulled
 1  c. sugar
 3  T. cornstarch
 2  T. lemon juice
    Whipped cream

In a saucepan, crush 1 pint hulled fresh strawberries with a fork or a pastry blender. Stir in sugar combined with cornstarch and lemon juice. Cook over moderate heat, stirring until clear and thick. Cool. Halve another pint of berries; fold into cooled mixture. Pour into crust. Refrigerate until well chilled. Garnish with whipped cream.

## FRUIT GLAZES FOR PIES, TORTES AND FLANS

### PINEAPPLE GLAZE

 1  16¼-oz. can crushed pineapple, drained
    (save juice)
 1  T. cornstarch
 1  T. sugar
 ½  t. vanilla
    Yellow food coloring

Mix cornstarch and sugar together. Stir in pineapple juice and cook until thick and clear, about 5 minutes. Remove from heat and add vanilla, pineapple and 1 or 2 drops of yellow food coloring. Cool and spread over cake or pie.

### BLUEBERRY GLAZE

| 1 c. water | 2 T. lemon juice |
| 2½ T. cornstarch | 1 pt. blueberries, |
| 1 c. sugar | washed |

Mix sugar and cornstarch together. Gradually add water and stir until smooth. Stir in ½ cup blueberries. Cook, stirring constantly, until thick and clear, about 5 minutes. When clear, add lemon juice. Cool. Arrange fruit on top of pie or cake. Add glaze. Chill until set.

### STRAWBERRY OR RASPBERRY GLAZE

 1  c. water
 2½ T. cornstarch
 1  c. sugar
 2  T. lemon juice
 1  pt. strawberries, washed and hulled
    (or 1 pint raspberries, washed)

Mix sugar and cornstarch together. Gradually add water and stir until smooth. Cook, stirring constantly, until thick and clear, about 5 minutes. When clear, add lemon juice and 1 or 2 drops of red food coloring. Cool. Arrange fruit on top of pie or cake. Add glaze. Chill until set.

## PECAN PIE

This southern treat is very rich, so why not compound your calories by serving each portion with a dollop of whipped cream. Tomorrow we diet.

1 9-inch unbaked pie shell
3 eggs, beaten
½ c. sugar
1 c. dark corn syrup
⅛ t. salt
1 t. vanilla
¼ c. melted butter or margarine
1 c. pecans

Add sugar and syrup to the beaten eggs. Then add salt, vanilla and melted butter. Place pecans in bottom of unbaked pie shell. Add filling and bake at 350° for 50 to 60 minutes. The nuts will rise to the top of the pie filling to form a brown crust.

### FOOLPROOF CRUST

¼ lb. butter or margarine, softened
1 c. flour
¼ t. salt

Cut flour and salt into butter and mix until a ball forms. Pat dough with hands into a 9-inch pie plate, mending if necessary and fluting edge if desired. Add filling and bake as directed.

For pie shell, prick generously with a fork and bake at 400° for 12 to 15 minutes or until golden brown.

## CHOCOLATE SILK PIE

This smooth-as-silk pie is a classic man pleaser.

1 9-inch baked pie shell
1 c. butter, softened
1½ c. sugar
4 squares baking chocolate, melted and cooled
4 eggs
1 t. vanilla
Whipped cream

Cream butter and sugar. Add chocolate and vanilla. Beat with electric mixer at low speed until well blended. Add eggs and beat 10 minutes. Pour into baked pie shell. Chill for about 3 hours. Top with whipped cream if desired. May be frozen.

## OLD-FASHIONED PUMPKIN PIE

Try a little of your best brandy in this never-fail traditional pumpkin pie.

1 9-inch unbaked pie shell
1 c. sugar
2 T. flour
½ t. salt
½ t. ground ginger
½ t. cinnamon
½ t. ground nutmeg
⅛ t. ground cloves
3 eggs
1½ c. pumpkin
2 c. milk (1 c. evaporated milk and 1 c. water)
1 T. brandy (optional)
Whipped cream
Pecans

Mix together sugar, flour, salt, ginger, cinnamon, nutmeg and cloves. Beat in eggs. Stir in pumpkin, milk and brandy. Pour into unbaked pie shell and bake in a preheated 400° oven 45 to 50 minutes or until a knife inserted in the center comes out clean. Cool and serve garnished with whipped cream and pecans.

## FRENCH APPLE PIE

Apple pie is the most popular pie in America, but this one is not like Grandma used to make.

### BOTTOM CRUST

Crumble and pat in bottom and sides of 9- or 10-inch pie plate:

1½ c. flour
6 T. butter
¼ t. salt

Combine and put in lined pie plate:

| | |
|---|---|
| 5 c. chopped pared apples | ¾ c. sugar |
| | 1 t. cinnamon |
| 1 T. lemon juice | ¼ t. salt |
| 3 T. flour | |

### TOP CRUST

| | |
|---|---|
| ½ c. butter | ⅛ t. salt |
| ½ c. brown sugar | 1 c. flour |

Cream butter, sugar and salt until fluffy. Cut in flour until lumps form, then sprinkle over top of pie. Bake at 375° for 55 minutes.

 # COOKIES

## DIAMOND HEAD DREAMS

A new way of putting things together.

½ c. butter              ½ t. salt
½ c. brown sugar     1 c. flour

Cream butter and sugar. Add flour and salt and mix until crumbly. Press into bottom of 9 x 13-inch pan. Bake in a preheated 350° oven for 12 to 15 minutes until golden brown.

### FILLING

3 eggs, well          1 t. vanilla
   beaten             ½ t. almond extract
1 c. brown sugar    1½ c. coconut
2 T. flour            ½ c. chopped nuts
½ t. salt                (optional)

Mix all together and spread on baked crust. Return to oven, bake 20 to 25 minutes until toothpick comes out clean. Cool for ½ hour and cut into bars or squares.

## MUD HENS

These puffy nut squares, topped with a dollop of whipped cream, will make dessert for a crowd. You will also like them "as is."

1 c. sugar              1 t. baking powder
¼ lb. butter or      ¼ t. salt
   margarine           1 t. vanilla
3 eggs                  2 c. brown sugar
1½ c. flour            1 c. chopped nuts

Cream butter and sugar until fluffy. Add 3 egg yolks and 1 egg white. Blend well. Add flour, baking powder and salt. Mix well. Add vanilla. Pat into a 10½ x 15½-inch greased jelly roll pan, using flour for your hands (dough will be sticky).

Cream brown sugar and 2 egg whites together and spread on dough. Sprinkle with nuts. Bake in a preheated 375° oven 20 to 25 minutes. It will be puffy. Cool for a few minutes before cutting into squares. Makes 35 large squares.

## FRENCH CREAM SLICES

A Napoleonic confection with the American touch of ease.

### FIRST LAYER

⅓ c. butter or margarine
¼ c. sugar
1 oz. baking chocolate
1 t. vanilla
1 egg, beaten
1½ c. graham cracker crumbs
½ c. chopped nuts
1 c. flaked coconut

Combine butter, sugar, chocolate in a saucepan or double boiler. Stir over low heat. Add vanilla and egg and simmer 5 minutes. Add crumbs, nuts and coconut. Press into a 9-inch square pan and chill 15 minutes.

The egg may be omitted and butter or margarine increased to ½ cup.

### SECOND LAYER

½ c. butter or margarine
2 T. instant French vanilla pudding mix
2 c. powdered sugar
3 T. milk

Cream butter, pudding mix, sugar and milk, beating until light and fluffy. Spread over chilled first layer. Chill again 15 minutes and prepare glaze.

### GLAZE

1 T. butter or margarine
4 ozs. semisweet chocolate

Melt butter with chocolate and spread over second layer. Chill and cut into 8 slices or small squares. Keep refrigerated or freeze.

## DATE BALLS

A nutritious nibble for health food enthusiasts. Wheat germ supplies the crunch.

3 ozs. cream cheese, softened
2 c. powdered sugar
1 c. snipped dates
½ t. salt
½ c. wheat germ
½ t. cinnamon

Mix sugar into softened cream cheese until smooth. Add dates and salt and mix well. Form into balls. Mix wheat germ and cinnamon together. Roll date balls in the mixture to coat. Chill. Makes 12 to 18 balls.

## LEMON BARS

These lemony little cakes are perfect for coffee time, tea time, party time, anytime.

2 c. sifted flour
½ c. powdered sugar, sifted
½ lb. butter or margarine

Sift flour and sugar. Cut in butter until mixture clings together. Press evenly into a 9 x 13-inch baking pan. Bake in a preheated 350° oven for 20 to 25 minutes or until lightly browned.

### FILLING

4 eggs, beaten
1 c. sugar
⅓ c. lemon juice
1 t. grated lemon rind
1 c. flaked coconut (optional in crust)
¼ c. flour
½ t. baking powder

To the beaten eggs add sugar combined with flour and baking powder, lemon juice and rind. Pour over baked crust and bake for 20 to 25 more minutes. Cut while warm. When cool sprinkle with powdered sugar or ice with the following glaze.

### GLAZE

½ c. powdered sugar
1 T. melted butter
1 T. lemon juice

Combine sugar with butter and lemon juice and beat until smooth. Spread lightly on bars.

## SCOTCH SHORTBREAD

In Scotland, shortbread is eaten with a glass of Scotch. Tea-time favorites with us, they will become a cookie tin favorite with you. But don't expect them to stay there long. No one can eat just one.

½ lb. butter          2 c. flour
½ c. sugar

Cream butter until very soft. Add sugar and beat until light and fluffy. Add flour ½ cup at a time, mixing well after each addition. Mix until all flour is blended and the bowl is clean. Press the mixture into an 8 x 12-inch ungreased cookie pan with hands to about ¼- to ½-inch thick. Bake at 350° for 30 minutes. It should be slightly brown when done and may be soft in the center. Score for cutting while warm, cut when cool. Makes 2 to 3 dozen shortbreads.

## PECAN TARTS

These bite-sized tarts are a show-off treat for a tea or ladies' luncheon.

### PASTRY

1 3-oz. pkg. cream cheese
½ c. butter or margarine
1 c. flour

Soften butter and cream cheese at room temperature. Blend and stir in flour. Chill slightly about 1 hour. Shape in 2 dozen 1-inch balls and place in ungreased tiny muffin cups. Press dough on bottom and sides of cups.

### FILLING

¾ c. brown sugar
1 egg
1 T. soft butter
1 t. vanilla
Dash of salt
½ c. chopped pecans
24 pecan halves

Beat together egg, sugar, butter, vanilla and salt until smooth. Add chopped nuts to mixture and fill pastry-lined cups. Top with pecan half. Bake at 325° for 25 minutes. Cool and remove from pans. Makes 24 tarts. Recipe may be doubled.

---

Shelled nuts should be refrigerated and will keep indefinitely in the freezer.

---

## DATE TORTE BARS

A sweet thought to send to students away from home. The recipe is so simple you'll want to make it often, and there are no bowls or beaters to wash.

¼ lb. butter            ½ c. chopped nuts
1 c. packed            ½ c. chopped dates
   brown sugar         1 t. vanilla
2 eggs, slightly        ½ t. soda
   beaten              ¼ t. salt
¾ c. flour

Melt butter in 8- or 9-inch pan. Remove from heat. Add remaining ingredients and beat with fork until mixture is smooth and creamy. Bake at 350° for 35 minutes. Cut in squares or bars. Sprinkle with powdered sugar if desired.

"The Gourmet Touch"
with
June Turner
and
Naomi Arbit

## KANELLA

These traditional Greek cookies are easy to make and keep indefinitely in a tightly covered container.

½ c. butter
½ c. granulated sugar
½ c. brown sugar, packed
1 egg
2 T. milk
1 t. vanilla
2¼ c. flour
1 t. baking powder
1 t. cinnamon
½ t. salt
1 c. ground walnuts

Cream butter and sugars. Add egg, milk, vanilla and beat well. Sift flour with baking powder, cinnamon and salt. Add to batter gradually, mixing well after each addition. Stir in nuts. Pinch off pieces about ½ teaspoonful, roll into a ball and flatten into ovals. Bake on a greased or nonstick cookie sheet in a pre-heated 350° oven 12 to 15 minutes. Makes 6 dozen. Roll in powdered sugar while hot.

## LACE WAFERS

These cookies are light and lacy. Do not try them on humid days, as they require dry air to become crisp.

½ c. sifted flour
½ c. shredded coconut
¼ c. brown sugar, packed
¼ c. butter or margarine
¼ c. dark corn syrup
½ t. vanilla

Combine flour and coconut. In a heavy sauce-pan melt butter, brown sugar and syrup. Bring to a boil. Remove from heat, blend in flour-coconut mixture. Add vanilla. Drop by scant teaspoonsful about 3 inches apart on an ungreased cookie sheet. Bake at 325° for 8 to 10 minutes.

Allow cookies to set for a few minutes before removing to rack covered with paper towels. If cookies are hard to remove, return to oven for a few seconds to soften. Makes about 2 dozen.

## STRUDEL

Traditional bakers spent the day pulling the dough to achieve the paper-thin flakiness needed for good strudel. Now you can have the same results with this quick never-fail method.

½ lb. butter or margarine
2 c. flour
¼ t. salt
1 c. sour cream

Cream butter, cut in flour and salt. Add sour cream and form into dough. Divide dough into 4 parts. Wrap each part in waxed paper and chill for several hours. Roll out dough to large rectangle on floured waxed paper. Don't be afraid to patch or mend.

### FILLING

1⅓ c. pineapple, orange or apricot marmalade
1 c. coconut
½ c. slivered maraschino cherries
1 c. snipped white raisins
1 c. chopped nuts

Spread dough with ⅓ cup marmalade and ¼ cup each of coconut, raisins, nuts and ⅛ cup cherries. Roll jelly-roll fashion, completely enclosing the filling.

Place each roll on a greased cookie sheet and slash top diagonally in desired width. Bake at 350° for 35 minutes until just golden. Quickly remove to waxed paper and slice. When cool, dust with powdered sugar. Makes 48 slices.

This dough may be filled with chopped liver (see appetizers section), baked and served as a hot hors d'oeuvre.

## SUGAR N' SPICE WALNUTS

. . . And everything nice because you don't use a candy thermometer for this treat.

1½ c. walnut halves
¼ c. sugar
1 T. cinnamon
⅛ t. ground cloves
⅛ t. nutmeg
1 egg white, beaten slightly

Coat nuts thoroughly in egg white, a few at a time. Mix sugar, cloves, cinnamon and nutmeg together. Drop nuts into mixture. Place on buttered cookie sheet or nonstick pan and bake in a preheated 300° oven for 30 minutes.

# INDEX

# IMAGE COMICS, INC.

**Robert Kirkman** — Chief Operating Officer
**Erik Larsen** — Chief Financial Officer
**Todd McFarlane** — President
**Marc Silvestri** — Chief Executive Officer
**Jim Valentino** — Vice President

**Eric Stephenson** — Publisher
**Corey Hart** — Director of Sales
**Jeff Boison** — Director of Publishing Planning & Book Trade Sales
**Chris Ross** — Director of Digital Sales
**Jeff Stang** — Director of Specialty Sales
**Kat Salazar** — Director of PR & Marketing
**Drew Gill** — Art Director
**Heather Doornink** — Production Director
**Branwyn Bigglestone** — Controller

## IMAGECOMICS.COM

RICH TOMMASO

# SPY SEAL
### BRITAIN'S SLICKEST SECRET AGENT

# THE CORTEN-STEEL PHOENIX

IMAGE COMICS
PORTLAND, OR

SPY SEAL, VOL I. THE CORTEN-STEEL PHOENIX. First printing. January 2018.
Published by Image Comics, Inc. Office of publication: 2701 NW Vaughn Street,
Suite 780, Portland, OR 97210. Copyright © 2018 Rich Tommaso. All rights reserved.
Contains material originally published in single magazine form as SPY SEAL #1-4.
SPY SEAL™ (including all prominent characters featured herein), its logo and all
character likenesses are trademarks of Rich Tommaso, unless otherwise noted.
Image Comics® and its logos are registered trademarks of Image Comics, Inc. No
part of this publication may be reproduced or transmitted, in any form or by any
means (except for short excerpts for review purposes) without the express written
permission of Rich Tommaso or Image Comics, Inc. All names, characters, events
and locales in this publication are entirely fictional. Any resemblance to actual
persons (living or dead), events or places, without satiric intent, is coincidental.
Printed in the USA. For information regarding the CPSIA on this printed material
call: 971-865-5786 and provide reference #RICH-768439. For international
rights, contact: foreignlicensing@imagecomics.com. ISBN: 978-1-5343-0479-6.

OH, YEAH?

YEAH, OKAY! LET'S GO LOOK AT SOME ART!

The PHOENIX GALLERY

WOW.

HE'S REALLY GREAT, ISN'T HE?

YEAH-- THIS IS AMAZING.

IT'S MODERN IN CONTENT AND STYLE, BUT IT FEELS LIKE IT WAS PAINTED CENTURIES AGO...VERY ROUGH, BUT BEAUTIFUL...STARK BRUSH STROKES...AND IT LOOKS LIKE IT'S VIBRATING...

YEAH-- HE DOES HAVE QUITE AN INCREDIBLE TECHNIQUE...VERY LOOSE, BUT WONDERFULLY STRUCTURED AT THE SAME TIME. SIGH...I WISH I COULD LOOSEN UP LIKE THIS...I JUST FEEL LIKE EVERYTHING I PAINT IS SO DAMN CONTROLLED--STIFF AND OVER-WORKED...

?

HELL—O?

DIS WORK VERY GOOD. ALL THIS—VERY NICE... YOU STAY FOR SHOW?

SHOW? OHHH, NO, I'M NOT AN ARTIST.

NO, NO—SHOW... PERFORMANCE SHOW UPSTAIRS.

OH—YEAH, I THINK SO.

IT STARTING SOON...

COME, WE GET SEATS...

UHHHHH— OH-KAY.

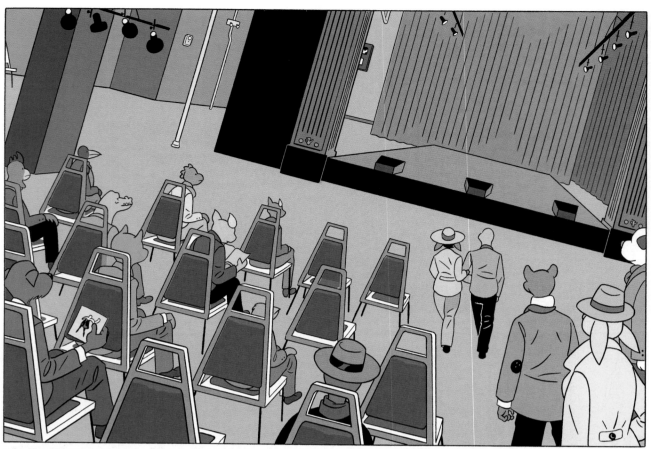

AHH—HERE IS GOOD.

IS OKAY I SIT WITH YOU? I AM ALONE TONIGHT. AND VERY NEW IN TOWN...

NO, NO—THAT'S PERFECTLY FINE.

SORRY!

A SULTRY, BUXOM BUNNY RABBIT? REALLY?

WHY DO YOU KEEP LOOKING AT THIS WOMAN BACK THERE? SHE IS YOUR GIRLFRIEND?

NO, NO—UHH, SHE'S JUST A DEAR FRIEND. WE CAME HERE TOGETHER, THAT'S ALL...

HMM...

HELLO, LOVE! COME SIT DOWN. THAT DIRTY LI'L SEAL OVER THERE JUST ABANDONED ME FOR A BIG, VOLUPTUOUS BUNNY!

OHH, FORGET THAT OL' RIVER RAT, MY DEAR. YOU'RE WITH A MEMBER OF PARLIAMENT NOW—HEH, HEH!

I'M SORRY. I JUST NEED YOU TO SIT WITH ME FOR A WHILE... I KNOW NO ONE IN THIS STRANGE CITY... YOU LIKE ME, NO?...

UHHH, YEAH... SURE.

SWOON

COME HERE, BIG BOY! LET ME LAY MY HEAD ON YOUR SHOULDER.

HA, HA! NOW, NOW, YOUNG LADY. I'M A MARRIED MAN!

AI-YI YI!

SHH! I KNOW THAT! I READ THE PAPERS! JUST PLAY ALONG, YA BIG GIRL'S BLOUSE!

HEH, HEH! OKAY!

LADIES AND GENTS, THANK YOU FOR JOINING US TONIGHT AT THE NEW PHOENIX GALLERY... WE HAVE SOME GREAT PERFORMANCES FOR YOU THIS EVENING AND WE ARE GRATEFUL AND PLEASED TO HAVE SUCH A WONDERFUL TURNOUT! ALSO, A ROUND OF APPLAUSE FOR ALL OF THE INCREDIBLE ARTISTS SHOWCASING THEIR FINE WORKS OF ART WITH US TONIGHT —

CLAP CLAP CLAP CLAP CLAP
CLAP CLAP CLAP CLAP CLAP

OKAY, NOW FIRST UP, AN ORIGINAL MODERN DANCE PERFORMANCE BY ARTISTS GELFER AND HELLMANN...

DEATH TO ALL IMPERIALIST PIG-DOGS!

SQWAK!!!

BANG

SYLVIA!

YIKES! THIS IS THE WORST PERFORMANCE ART PIECE I'VE EVER SEEN IN MY ENTIRE LIFE!

BLAM!

ACK!

ARE YOU OKAY?

YEAH--I I THINK SO...

JUST WINGED ME--HEH!

CRACK!

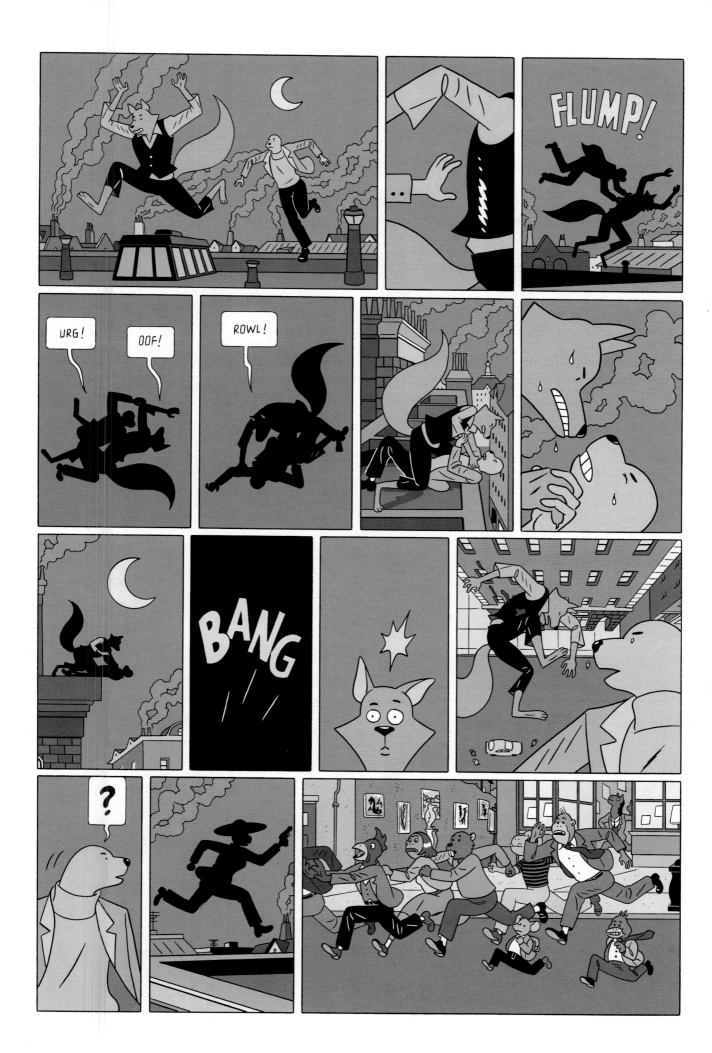

WELL, WELL! LOOK WHO IT IS!

WHAT YOU DID WAS VERY BRAVE, MY BOY. I CANNOT THANK YOU ENOUGH! LEAPING OVER THOSE CHAIRS LIKE THAT--LIKE A CHEETAH! I'M VERY GRATEFUL TO YOU.

PHOOOO... WELL, I JUST DID WHAT I THOUGHT I HAD TO DO...

HONESTLY, I WAS ONLY TRYING TO PROTECT MY DEAR OL' FRIEND, SYL HERE...

MY MAN MALCOLM. I KNEW YOU'D COME BACK TO ME IN THE END!

I UNDERSTAND, BUT NOT MANY WOULD STAND IN THE LINE OF FIRE THAT WAY, EVEN FOR A FRIEND. AND, ALBEIT INADVERTENT, YOU DID PROTECT ME AS WELL--AND INCAPACITATED THE ASSASSINS.

TOOK ONE OF 'EM OUT.

I SAW THAT YOU GOT THE GUNMAN. HE'S LYING DEAD IN THE STREET, 'ROUND THE CORNER.

NOT ME, I'M AFRAID--IT WAS SOMEONE ELSE WHO DID THE SHOOTING-- I WAS FIGHTING HIM HAND TO HAND WHEN THE SHOT RANG OUT...

I COULDN'T QUITE SEE, BUT I BELIEVE IT WAS THE SAME WOMAN WHO DISARMED HIM AT THE ART SHOW EARLIER... I'M GRATEFUL--WHOEVER IT WAS--HE WAS CLOSE TO GIVING ME THE HEAVE-HO OFF OF A VERY HIGH LEDGE!

NO WORRIES, MY BOY...AND NO NEED TO EXPLAIN--HE WAS A RED SPY WHO CAME TO A STICKY END, THAT'S ALL.

WE'LL VOUCH FOR YOU.

THANK YOU, I APPRECIATE THAT. NOW, IF YOU WILL PLEASE EXCUSE US...

OF COURSE.

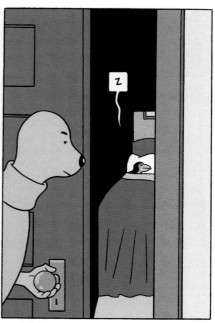

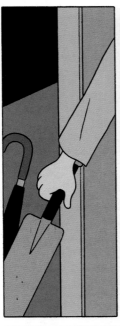
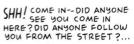

AND--I'M HOLDING SECRET VITAL TO THIS COUNTRY'S SAFETY! THIS IS WHY MEN ARE AFTER ME...AND THESE MEN, THEY WILL STOP AT NOTHING!

SOUNDS LIKE A SPY NOVEL TO ME...

EXACTLY. BUT I PREFER SECRET AGENT.

BRITISH AGENT, YES? WOULD YOU CARE FOR SOME TEA, MISS...?

YOU CAN CALL ME ANGORA. AND YES TO BOTH.

I HAVE TO SAY, THERE ARE LIMITS TO THE FREEDOMS IN MY MOTHER COUNTRY AS WELL MISS ANGORA.

HA! YOU DO NOT KNOW WHAT IT IS LIKE! YOU GIVE UP LITTLE FREEDOMS HERE, MEANINGLESS. YOU NOT JAILED OR KILLED FOR SPEAKING YOUR MIND!

WELL, I CAN HARDLY DISAGREE WITH YOU THERE. BUT AS FAR AS GOVERNMENTS ARE RUN, THEY ALL RESORT TO VIOLENCE AT ONE POINT OR ANOTHER.

ACH! THIS IS QUIBBLING OVER LITTLE DETAILS. I JUST WANT TO BE FREE--AND FOR THAT I NEED MONEY, FROM HIGHEST BIDDER. RIGHT NOW, THAT IS BRITAIN...

MMM, I SEE... AND THEN WHAT? MAKE YOUR WAY ABROAD, TO THE STATES? OR DO YOU MOVE IN WITH ME?

HA, I'M SORRY! I JUST NEED TO STAY HERE A WHILE, UNTIL THOSE MEN GO AWAY...

MEN?

OUTSIDE. SEE FOR YOURSELF.

eeee

eeeee

eee

WHY DID YOU KILL ANGORA?! SHE WASN'T A RED SPY-- JUST THE OPPOSITE!

I AM WELL AWARE OF THAT, YOUNG MAN!

AS I JUST STATED, WE ARE WITH MI-6 AND ANGORA WAS WORKING FOR US--WE DIDN'T KILL HER--TWO MEN ON YOUR ROOFTOP SHOT HER... MOSTLY LIKE AGENTS OF THE RUSSIAN SECRET SERVICE...WE HEARD THE SHOTS OUTSIDE AND HOOFED IT RIGHT OVER HERE.

I DIDN'T SEE ANY MEN OUT THERE, ACTUALLY--BUT HERE YOU TWO ARE, IN A FLASH.

SIR! MI-6 ARE NOT IN THE HABIT OF NEUTRALIZING OUR OWN OPERATIVES! WE WERE IN CLOSE PROXIMITY BECAUSE WE'D FOLLOWED YOU HOME AFTER THAT WHOLE INCIDENT YOU'D GOTTEN YOURSELF WRAPPED UP IN!

SO, DID SHE SAY ANYTHING TO YOU? WHAT'S THAT YOU HAVE THERE?

IT'S A PIN--SHE SAID SOMETHING ABOUT A CORTEN-STEEL PHOENIX. SHE ALSO SAID THE GALLERY WAS INVOLVED SOMEHOW IN THE SHOOTING TONIGHT.

IS THIS IT? THE CORTEN-STEEL PHOENIX?

NO, THAT'S NOT CORTEN STEEL, THAT'S A CLOISONNÉ PIN.

AH--YOU KNOW A LOT ABOUT ART TOO, HUH?

NOT REALLY. MOST OF IT IS SECOND-HAND KNOWLEDGE THROUGH MY ARTIST BUDDY, SYLVIA--THE BIRD WHO WAS ALSO SHOT EARLIER TONIGHT...

OOF! AND HE ALSO KNOWS HOW TO SWING A BAT! NICE CRACK, OLD MAN...

YES, YES--YOU DO HANDLE YOURSELF QUITE WELL, MR.--MR.--?

WARNER--MALCOLM WARNER...YES, I SUPPOSE MY STINT IN THE MILITARY TAUGHT ME SOME THINGS ABOUT DEFENDING MYSELF. ALSO, I PRACTICE JIU-JITSU.

DOESN'T SURPRISE ME IN THE LEAST. TELL ME, MALCOLM...

EVER THOUGHT OF BECOMING A SPY?

OHH...

I DON'T KNOW...

EMERGENCY!

RIGHT HERE...

ME? A SPY?

WHY NOT? YOU HAVE THE DEMEANOR. YOU HAVE ALL OF THE QUALITIES... AND--WE DON'T ALL END UP LIKE POOR ANGORA.

I MAY HAVE THE DEMEANOR, BUT NOT THE STATUS. I HAPPEN TO BE BROKE AT THE MOMENT.

NO WORRIES ABOUT ALL THAT, MALCOLM. IF YOU DECIDE TO JOIN US, WE'LL SET YOU UP WITH A JOB STRAIGHT AWAY. I HAVE JUST THE THING IN MIND RIGHT NOW, IN FACT...

REALLY? WELL, THAT'S ENCOURAGING.

HERE, MY BOY--TAKE MY CARD... AND IF YOU'RE INTERESTED, GIVE US A CALL...

YOU KNOW SIR, I JUST MAY DO THAT...

BZZZZZZZ

BZZZZZZ

DING
DING
DING

OH--

GOOD MORNING, SIR!

GOOD MORNING, YOUNG LADY.

CAN I HELP YOU WITH ANYTHING?

OH, JUST LOOKING AROUND AT SOME POTENTIAL ACQUISITIONS THAT'S ALL...

AH--WELL, LET ME KNOW IF YOU HAVE ANY QUESTIONS OR IF THERE'S ANYTHING I CAN SHOW YOU FROM OUR PRIVATE COLLECTION.

THANK YOU. I SHALL!

EXCUSE ME--

I MOSTLY COLLECT PAINTINGS--UHH, HERE, MY CARD--

TERRY FALCONER
ART DEALER
NYC · LONDON

BUT I AM INTRIGUED BY THAT GLORIOUS BIRD SCULPTURE OVER THERE!

WHAT IS THE PRICE ON THAT ITEM, IF I MAY ASK?

THE PHOENIX FIGURINE...

YES.

MHMM-- THAT ITEM, I AM AFRAID --

TOSS

IS NOT FOR SALE... IF I MAY ASK?... SIR.

OH...OH, REALLY? SHAME...

SO SORRY.

MMM--YESSS, I'M SURE YOU ARE, MY DEAR FOWL--NO MATTER...

SNAP

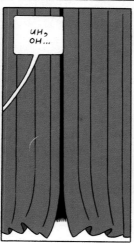
UH, OH...

FOR YOU, MONSIEUR!

EH?

OH--UH, THANK YOU, SIR.

CERTAINEMENT.

ROYAL OFFICE
TELEGRAM
RECEIVED
Charges to pay
3/64
PREFIX 33
From
3.64 MALCOLM GOOD WORK + BUT
NEED TO RE ROUTE MISSION +++ THE
ENEMY HAS BEEN ROUSTED
STAY IN HOTEL TAPIOCA AND
AWAYT FURTHER INSTRUCTIONS +
J.B. COLLINS +++
SPEAK SHORTLY

TELEGRAMS ENQUIRY ** or call

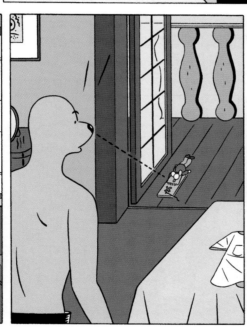

MALCOLM?

MISSION HERE IS OVER, AGENT 001!--

SO, THE BOYS AT THE NEST ARE SENDING YOU HELP--BUT YOU'LL HAVE TO LEAVE THIS LOCATION NOW--IT'S NOT SAFE--THE BAD BOYS PROBABLY KNOW WHO YOU ARE AND WHERE YOU'RE STAYING BY THIS POINT...

CRIKEY! YES, I WAS TOLD THINGS WENT BELLY-UP AND THAT I WAS TO STAY PUT UNTIL FURTHER NOTICE--GUESS I REALLY MUCKED THINGS UP, HUH?

S'ALL RIGHT--IT'S YOUR VERY FIRST MISSION--BUT, YEAH, YOU SHOULDN'T HAVE ASKED ABOUT THE STATUE--THEY'VE BEEN RUMBLED--CLOSED UP SHOP, PACKED UP, MOVED OUT--TODAY...WE *DID* GRAB THE STATUE THOUGH, DON'T WORRY 'BOUT THAT...

CHEERS. HOW'D YOU DO THAT?

AT 1400 HOURS, YOU'LL GO TO GRACE GARDENS TO MEET YOUR CONTACT. SHE'LL GUIDE YOU THROUGH THE REST OF THIS OPERATION. A VERY EXPERIENCED AGENT, KES--BEEN WITH THE AGENCY FOR YEARS...SHE'LL FILL YOU IN ON ALL OF THE DETAILS OF THE PAST COUPLE OF DAYS AND HOW YOU'LL BE MOVING FORWARD.

EXCELLENT, EXCELLENT.

UHHHH-- WHAT DOES SHE LOOK LIKE?

KES. SHE'S A KESTREL, AIN'T SHE?

OH-- RIGHT.

F-WOOSH

YES, I WAS IN A HURRY, WASN'T I? A BIT TOO EAGER TO PROVE MYSELF...AND STUPIDLY SHOWED MY HAND TO THE ENEMY IN THE PROCESS...

OBSERVE AND ASSESS BEFORE YOU ENGAGE, MALCOLM.

A TIGHT LIP IS KEY WHEN YOU'VE GOT AN ENEMY WHO'S ALREADY PARTIALLY EXPOSED AND ON THEIR GUARD.

GOOD ADVICE.

AND BOY ARE YOU GORGEOUS!

THAT'S WHAT I'M HERE FOR... I'LL BE WITH YOU FROM NOW ON -- USUALLY, ON THE FIRST GO 'ROUND, THE NEST WILL SEND AN AGENT OUT IN THE FIELD ALONE -- TO TEST OUT THEIR ABILITY -- SEE WHAT THEY CAN DO ON INSTINCT.

I FAILED THAT TEST PRETTY QUICKLY -- I'M NOT A NATURAL AT THIS GAME I GUESS.

IT'S NOT EASY FOR ANY SPY IN THE BEGINNING, TRUST ME...EVERY NEW RECRUIT EVENTUALLY NEEDS THE ASSISTANCE OF A SEASONED AGENT ON THEIR VERY FIRST MISSION...

ALSO, NO ONE GOES IT ALONE ON A MISSION AS BIG AS THIS, SO DON'T WORRY ABOUT IT...I MUST SAY, YOU DID A CRACKING-GOOD JOB GETTING AWAY FROM THOSE TWO THUGS -- SO YOU DO HANDLE YOURSELF WELL, WHICH IS WHY YOU WERE CHOSEN FOR FIELD WORK IN THE FIRST PLACE...

SO, WHO CLEANED UP MY MESS, WAS IT YOU?

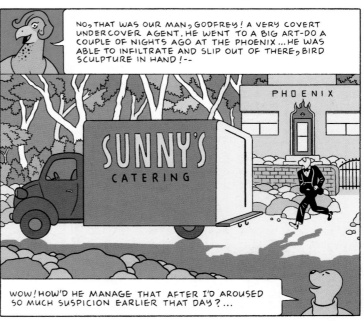

NO, THAT WAS OUR MAN, GODFREY! A VERY COVERT UNDERCOVER AGENT. HE WENT TO A BIG ART-DO A COUPLE OF NIGHTS AGO AT THE PHOENIX...HE WAS ABLE TO INFILTRATE AND SLIP OUT OF THERE, BIRD SCULPTURE IN HAND!--

PHOENIX

SUNNY'S CATERING

WOW! HOW'D HE MANAGE THAT AFTER I'D AROUSED SO MUCH SUSPICION EARLIER THAT DAY?...

YOU KNOW, IT WAS ACTUALLY QUITE EASY. IT SHOULDN'T HAVE BEEN, BUT BY A SHEER STROKE OF LUCK, IN THE FORM OF A PUBLIC PROTEST, HE WAS ABLE TO COMPLETE THIS TASK WITH RELATIVE EASE...

DING DING DING

*ВНИМАНИЕ!

THESE THREE RABBIT RUFFIANS CRASHED THE ART SHOW AND STARTED SPRAY-PAINTING EVERY PIECE OF ART IN THE PLACE!

* ATTENTION!

 DOWN WITH THE PHOENIX! DOWN WITH THEM AND THEIR RED ARMY!

 CRIKEY! WHAT A ODD BIT OF LUCK FOR GODFREY THEN, EH?... SO, MORE RUSSIAN DOUBLE AGENTS YOU THINK?

 NAH, SOUNDED MORE LIKE JUST A BUNCH OF HOOLIGANS TO ME, BUT BY JOVE, DID THEY HELP US GET WHAT WE WANTED! GODFREY WAS ABLE TO MOVE FAST, NICK THAT STATUE AND BOOK IT OUTTA THERE, TOOT SWEET.

BRILLIANT, BUT I WONDER WHAT'S INSIDE OF IT?

 IT'S ANOTHER OBJECT THAT ISN'T MADE OF CORTEN-STEEL. YET, THAT BUNCH AT THE GALLERY WERE VERY AGITATED WHEN I ASKED ABOUT IT...

 COULD BE PLANS, MAYBE COORDINATES TO BRITISH MILITARY BASES--OR FACTORIES...BUT, IT COULD ALSO BE NOTHING--WHO KNOWS? YOU MIGHT'VE JUST SPOOKED THEM BY POINTING IT OUT OF THE LINE UP LIKE THAT. SINCE THEY'VE ALREADY HAD TO FLEE THEIR LONDON SET-UP AFTER THAT WHOLE MESS THAT WENT DOWN OUT THERE, THEY'RE PARANOID OVER ANYONE ASKING TO BUY A PHOENIX-SHAPED PIECE OF ART. IN ANY CASE, OUR TIME IS FINISHED HERE--TIME FOR US TO PRESS ON TO OUR NEXT DESTINATION...

WHERE TO NOW, KES?

 BELGIUM. ONE BY AIR, ONE BY LAND...WE NEED TO SPLIT UP FOR A FEW HOURS. TONIGHT YOU'LL FLY YOUR AIRPLANE INTO ITALY AND I'LL MEET UP WITH YOU--I'LL BE GOING BY TRAIN. YOU'LL FLY TO THESE COORDINATES--YOU WILL DITCH THE SEA PLANE AT A PRIVATE AIR FIELD--IN ITALY--AND MEET ME AT THE VICOMORASSO TRAIN STATION NEARBY...GOT IT?

Fly 14.2 km

 YES--FLY OVER THE BORDER, LAND IN GENOA, MEET YOU AT VICOMORASSO TRAIN STATION HERE. I GOT IT. THANK YOU, KES...

 NO PROBLEM. SEE YOU TONIGHT.

WHACK!

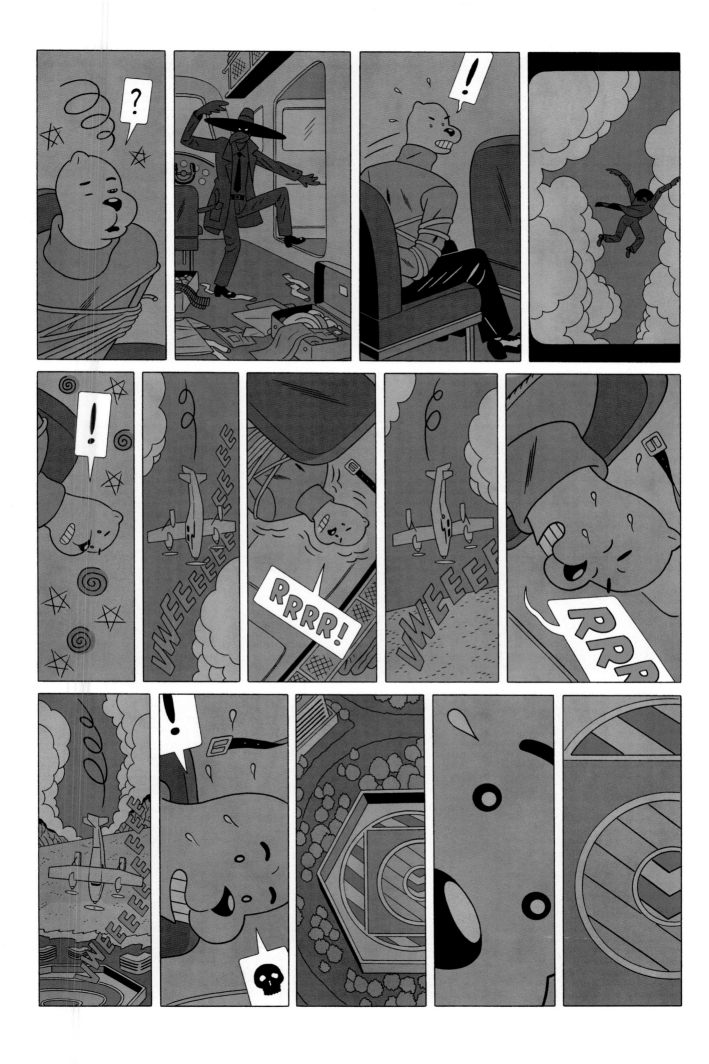

ALL ABOARD!

SHUFF SHUFF SHUFF

WAIT! WAIT!

!

HERE I COME!

WHUP!

!

OOF!

UHHHH--

WHOOPS!

WELL, I MADE IT!

GOOD SHOW! WE BETTER HURRY TO OUR NEXT TRAIN--IN LUCERNE--

ONE OF OUR SPY PLANES WAS JUST SHOT DOWN OVER ANTWERP.

SEE THIS GUY, MILES MCKELLER? HE'S WHO WE BELIEVE IS BEHIND ALL OF THIS. IN THE EARLY DAYS, LEADING UP TO THE WAR, HE MARCHED IN RALLIES FOR THE WORKERS PARTY, SO HE DEFINITELY HAD COMMUNIST TIES-- BUT BEING A COMMUNIST WASN'T A PROBLEM BACK WHEN WE WERE BUSY FIGHTING NAZIS.

SO, MI-6 LOOKED PAST MCKELLER'S COMMUNIST BACKGROUNDS WHEN HE WAS BEING CONSIDERED FOR EMPLOYMENT AT THE NEST.

MMM, AND SO YOU THINK THAT ALL OF THESE TERRORIST ATTACKS ARE HIM? WHY?

10 YEARS AGO, MI-6 FOUND OUT THAT HE'D BEEN WORKING AS A DOUBLE-AGENT FOR RUSSIA...

MILES WAS CAUGHT TELEGRAPHING SECRET INFORMATION ABOUT OUR AGENTS PLANTED IN BERLIN... HE WAS THROWN IN PRISON BUT THEN HE BROKE OUT SOMEHOW, FLED THE COUNTRY... MOST LIKELY HE EMIGRATED TO RUSSIA.

HMMM...

MILES MCKELLER.

LOOKS LIKE THE BIRD WHO CONKED ME ON THE HEAD LAST NIGHT.

KISS ME QUICK!

HUH?!

GRAB

MMMWAH!!!

GOOD HEAVENS! THAT WAS HIM!

SWAK!

WHA-?

THAT WAS HIM--MCKELLER!

ARE YOU HAVIN' A LAUGH?

I'M NOT! WHAT SHOULD WE DO? SHOULD WE GO AFTER HIM?

OR SHOULD WE GET OUT OF HERE? BEFORE HE RECOGNIZES ME?

YOU?

WHAT ABOUT ME? YOU THINK HE RECOGNIZED ME? HE ONLY SAW MY FACE JUST LAST NIGHT!

I KNOW-- SO WHAT SHALL WE DO? MAYBE WE SHOULD DITCH THIS TRAIN AND I COULD FLY US THE REST OF THE WAY? OR SHOULD WE JUST GO AFTER THE NASTY LITTLE SABOTEUR?

MALCOLM?

I-I'M SORRY--I'M STILL JUST A BIT FLUMMOXED AFTER ALL THAT SNOGGING!

MALCOLM! LEAVE IT OUT! WE'RE ON A MISSION HERE... THIS IS IMPORTANT...NOW, BE PROFESSIONAL!

COME ON--

WE NEED TO FIND THAT BIRD!

LUGGAGE

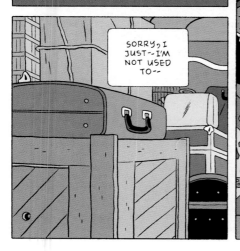

SORRY, I JUST--I'M NOT USED TO--

MALCOLM, YOU NEED TO CONCENTRATE--YOU MUST LEARN TO CONTROL YOUR EMOTIONS IF YOU'RE GOING TO DO THIS JOB...THERE ARE MANY...UNUSUAL THINGS YOU'LL HAVE TO DO TO GET OUT OF TIGHT JAMS WHILE OUT ON A MISSION...I'M NOT GOING TO BE THE ONLY WOMAN YOU'LL HAVE TO KISS, SEDUCE, OR SHACK UP WITH, IF NECESSARY...BUT YOU HAVE TO BE COOL ABOUT IT--COLD, MEAN, AND EMOTIONALLY DETACHED... YOU MUST DO THESE AND OTHER UNSAVORY THINGS UNFLINCHINGLY...AS SPIES WE MUST WEAR MANY FACES, MALCOLM.

'EY!

MANY FACES, THAT'S IT! WE SHOULD DRESS UP IN DISGUISES AND HIDE FROM THAT BIRD 'TIL WE'RE OFF THIS TRAIN. WHEN HE DEPARTS WE CAN FOLLOW HIM AND SEE WHERE HE GETS OFF TO!

LET'S DO IT!

SNAP!

WORTH A SHOT--

ACK!

POP!

THAT WAS YOU LAST NIGHT!

I SHOULD'VE SHOT YOU!

HERE'S A SHOT FOR YOUR FACE!

CRACK!

DIRTY TRAITOR!

ENOUGH! BACK OFF!--NOW!

WISH...

GO ON--BACK UP!--AND OPEN THAT DOOR!

EXIT

'EY-UP! NEED A LIFT?

WELKOM FLUPKE

CIVILIZATION! 'EY, KES?

YEAH, NICE BUT--

WHAT ON EARTH IS GOING ON HERE?

WITH WHAT? WHERE?

I'VE JUST SEEN FOUR SPIES WHO WERE SENT INTO THE COLD BY MI-6 YEARS AGO! WHAT ARE WE HEADING INTO? A DISGRUNTLED EX-SPY CONVENTION?

REALLY?

THERE'S ANOTHER ONE!--

THAT FOX!

AND ANOTHER!

AND TURTLE DOVE!

MAYBE THEY'RE ON THE JOB AGAIN? THIS ONE, YEAH?--

MNN-- I DOUBT THAT. MOST OF THESE GUYS HAVEN'T BEEN IN THE FIELD SINCE BEFORE THE WAR, MALCOLM.

THIS IS MAKING ME VERY NERVOUS. I'M FEELING EXTREMELY EXPOSED.

WELL, LET'S HIGH-TAIL IT TO THE HOTEL THEN!

NO MEAT?! I TELL YOU, IS THAT PROGRESS? IS THAT ORGANIZATION?!

I THINK THIS IS THE BEST ALE I'VE EVER TASTED!

YES, MAKES UP FOR THE LACK OF ACTUAL SOLID FOOD IN THIS PLACE.

THERE'RE SOME STALE ROLLS.

THEY SAID THIS IS HOW IT GOES WHENEVER THERE'S A BIG SNOW FALL IN THE HARSH WINTER MONTHS.

FOOD TRUCKS CAN'T GET TO TOWN -- THAT TRAIN MADE IT, THOUGH, BUT WE DIDN'T SEE MCKELLER HOP OFF IT.

MAYBE HE'LL BE AT THIS ART SHOW TONIGHT, EH?

'BOUT THAT-- PURLEY AND I SHOULD JUST GO IT ALONE, RIGHT? I MEAN, YOU LOT HAVE BEEN TOO EXPOSED NOW, YEAH?

YEAH, AFTER OUR TUSSLE WITH HIM I'D SAY MALCOLM AND I SHOULD DEFINITELY SIT THIS ONE OUT.

ALSO, I'VE SPOTTED MANY FAMILIAR FACES HERE IN FLUPKE THAT MAKE ME WANT TO HIDE MINE AS MUCH AS POSSIBLE.

RIGHT, YOU MENTIONED THAT EARLIER.

WE'LL KEEP IN CONTACT BY THE WIRELESS... IF THINGS GET OUT OF CONTROL WE CAN JUMP INTO THE BREACH IF NEED BE.

WORKS FOR US--I'M SURE WE'LL BE ABLE TO HANDLE IT ALONE...

BY THE WAY, THIS LITTLE GUY HERE? WAS ANALYZED BY OUR MAN HALFORD BACK AT THE NEST LABS.

AND?

NUTHIN'!

HMPH--STILL LEAVES US WITH THE MYSTERY OF THIS CORTEN-STEEL BIRD...PERHAPS IT'S A LANDMARK? BECAUSE CORTEN-STEEL SUGGESTS A RATHER LARGE PIECE OF ART... PERHAPS IT'S THE LANDMARK OF MCKELLER'S HOME BASE?

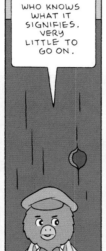

WHO KNOWS WHAT IT SIGNIFIES. VERY LITTLE TO GO ON.

TRUE...WELL, OFF YOU POP-- GO LOOK AT SOME ARTWORK BOYS...WE'LL BE IN TOUCH ON THE RADIO UPSTAIRS.

NIGHTY, NIGHT, CHAPS.

GOODNIGHT, MR. & MRS. WARNER!

CRUNCH!
MUNCH!
CRUNCH!
MUNCH!
CRUNCH!
MUNCH!

HAVING A SMASHING TIME, GODFREY?

ABOUT AS DULL AS CAN BE... NOT MUCH GOING ON AT ALL--

DON'T SEE ANYONE HERE WE KNOW, EXCEPT FOR THAT DESK CLERK IN MONACO. NOT THAT DRAGON LADY OR THOSE GOONS OF HERS...NOR IS THERE ANY SIGN OF McKELLER.

THOSE EX-SPIES THAT YOU SPOKE OF? TOOK A GOOD LOOK AROUND, DIDN'T SEE ANY FAMILIAR FACES... ONLY A BUNCH OF NOSES IN THE AIR, THAT'S ALL, KESSIE...

WHAT SHOULD WE DO? HEAD BACK?

MMM--GIVE IT ANOTHER HOUR, OKAY? AFTER THAT YOU CAN HEAD BACK.

10/4.

SOUNDS LIKE WE'VE POSSIBLY CHASED A WILD GOOSE HERE.

YOU COULD BE RIGHT SPY SEAL. NO SUSPICIOUS CHARACTERS AT THIS ART-DO...

DAMN! WE'LL NEED A NEW LEAD NOW, EY?

YES, BUT LOOKS LIKE TOMORROW WE'RE ON A FLIGHT BACK TO LONDON.

IT'S BEDDY-BYES FOR US, "HUSBAND"...I'M GETTING READY TO TURN IN ...

ALL RIGHT.

OKAY, ALL YOURS!

WHOAAA THIS BED FEELS GOOD!

OKAY, MAYBE I'LL TAKE A NICE, COLD SHOWER!

SLAM!

SILLY GOOSE.

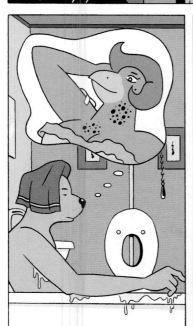

YOU'RE UNBELIEVABLE! YOU DON'T WANT ME AS A MATE--EVEN THOUGH WE'VE KNOWN EACH OTHER FOR AGES AND GET ON SO WELL TOGETHER--BUT YOU'RE IMMEDIATELY HEAD OVER HEELS FOR THAT TOUGH-AS-NAILS SPY IN THERE?

IT'S BECAUSE SHE'S BIG AND BUSTY, ISN'T IT? YOU DEFINITELY HAVE A TYPE, DON'T YOU? WELL, MALCOLM DEAR, YOU BEST FORGET ABOUT YOUR ROMANTIC LOVE NOTIONS AND JUST DO AS SHE'S TOLD YOU TO DO: GET AHOLD OF YOUR EMOTIONS AND BE PROFESSIONAL!

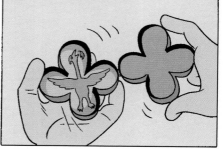
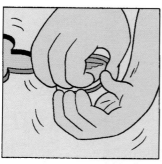

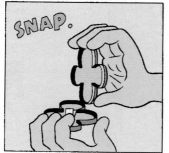

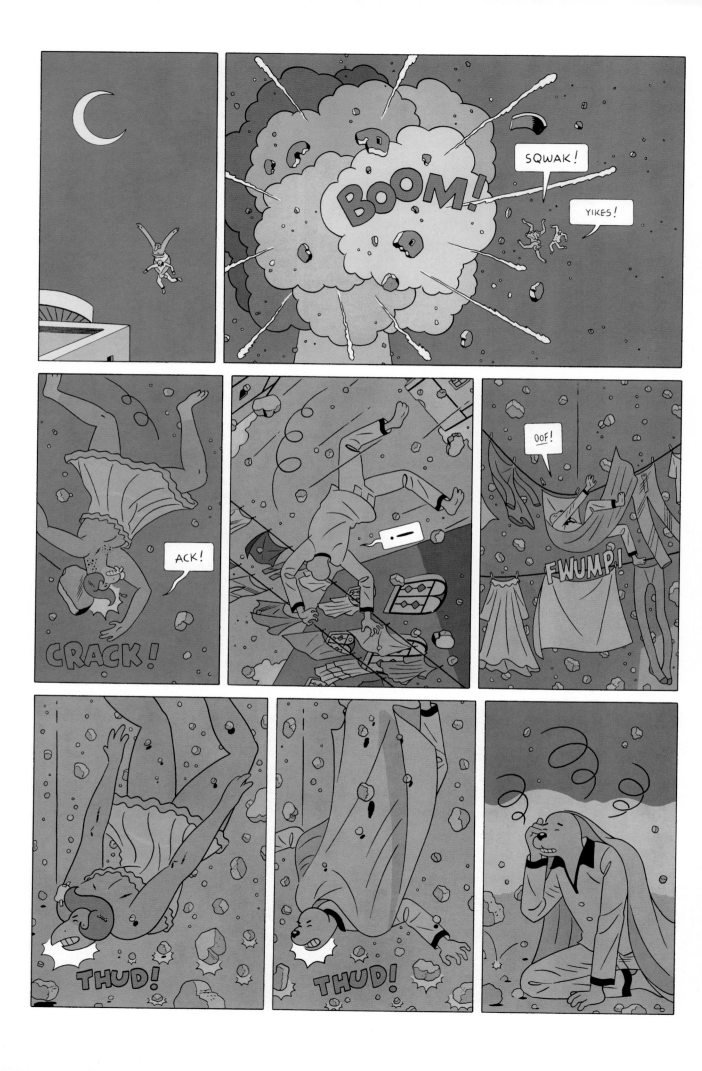

WELCOME, YE PEWR BODACH! COME IN FROM DE RAEN, LEMME GET YE SOMMAT TE DRINK...

PLEASE DO. PINT O' ALE MY GOOD DUCK--

AYE, SUR--COMIN' RIGHT UP.

DAER YE ARE, OL' MAN.

TA.

IT'S FAIR JEELIT OWT DAER, INNIT? Y'LOOK QUITE DROOKIT.

AYE, IT'S REALLY DREICH OWT T'NITE SOAKED TO ME BONES, I AM...

TELL ME, HAVE YE ANY ROOMS TO LET HERE?

OH, AYE--GOT ONE OPEN--LEFF, TOP O' DE STAIRS. WHAER'RE YOU OFF TAE ON THIS ILL NICHT?

BIG CASTLE, SOME'ERES...'POSED TO START AS GARD'NER UP DERE, ONLY 'AVE THIS WEE MAP TO GO BAE--

GIVE US A LOOK AT THAT--JINGS! THAT IS WEE TINY, INNIT?

AYE.

Wallace Blackwood 57° / 5.5

AH--THASS BLACKWOOD CASTLE, THAT IS! YE NOE FAR FROM DAT, I CAN TELL YE. THASS A LI'L WALK AND A SHORT RUN O'ER DE SEA... 'BOUT FIVE MILE JAUNT ALL T'GETHER.

OH, AYE? WELL, MAYBE I'LL JUST RUN ALONG OWT DERE NOW DEN?

NOO, NOO--YER MAD, MON! GOO OUT? IN DIS MESS? HOE YE 'ERE SEE ANYTHIN'? STAY DE NICHT--AYE'LL GIVE YUH GOOD RATE ON ROOM... DEN YE KIN FINISH YE JERRNIE T'MORRAH MOORN...

WHAT YE GONE DOO OWP DERE T'NITE ANYHOO? PROONE DERE WEE TREES WIFF A LANTERN?

AYE, YER RICHT--I AIN'T HALF-TIRED ANYWEE...

SOO, WHAT YE GOT TE EAT IN DIS TAVERN DEN?...

MS. SHINGLEBACH...

LLAZAR...

AUGUSTUS...

THIS IS PAMELA CARROLL, FORMER MI-6 AGENT.

OH, I'VE HEARD OF *YOU*...

YOU LOST A LOVED ONE DURING YOUR STINT WITH MI-6, HMM? THAT HURT YOUR WORK PERFORMANCE AFTERWARDS, EH?

YES--

WELL, WELCOME TO BLACKWOOD CASTLE...

AND--DO YOU HAVE SOMETHING FOR ME?

YES...

HERE YOU ARE.

ENJOY OUR PRIVATE COLLECTION, COMRADE.

THANK YOU.

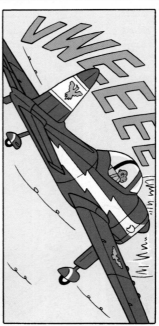

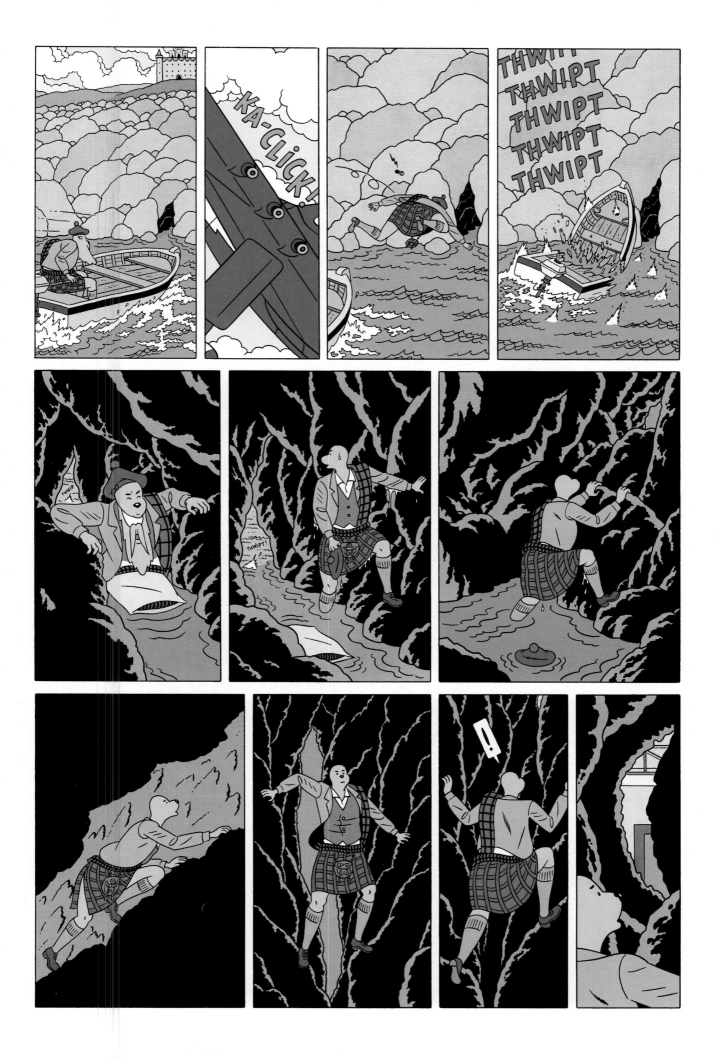

JACKPOT! THIS IS IT, BY JOVE--

THAT'S RIGHT, GOV'NAH-- THE WHOLE BLOODY LOT OF 'EM!

WHAT THE--?

OH, NO-- NOT *YOU*!

CONTROL? MUCH SMALLER GROUP AT THIS PARTY--IT'S ALL EX-AGENTS HERE--I FEEL LIKE THE TROUBLE AT THOSE PUBLIC ART SHOWS WAS A SET-UP TO THROW US OFF TRACK...AGENTS WERE PASSING INFO BACK AND FORTH--BUT I THINK THIS IS WHERE THAT INFO MEETS ITS FINAL DESTINATION--THIS HAS TO BE THEIR BASE OF OPERATIONS...

HMM--INTEL PASSED FROM OUR BOYS TO THE RUSSIANS, VIA INNOCUOUS ART SHOWS ALL ACROSS EUROPE--CLEVER... HIDDEN NEATLY INSIDE PHOENIX TRINKETS...

WE NEVER GOT OUR HANDS ON ANY OF 'EM BEFORE THEIR SECRETS HAD BEEN REMOVED--NEVER UNDERSTOOD THE PURPOSE OF THOSE FIGURINES UNTIL MALCOLM FOUND ANGORA'S LITTLE MAP...THAT'S WHEN WE REALISED WHAT THEY WERE USED FOR--I JUST USED ONE MYSELF TO GET IN HERE.

MMM, GOOD SHOW...BUT WHAT ABOUT MALCOLM? WHERE IS HE? I'VE LOST ALL CONTACT WITH HIM...

HE--HASN'T MADE IT HERE... THERE WAS A FIRE FIGHT OUT AT SEA--HE MUST'VE BEEN FOUND OUT--FUNNY, IT HASN'T SPOILED THE PARTY--I--I HOPE THEY HAVEN'T--ELIMINATED HIM...

WELL, IF NO ONE'S FEATHERS ARE RUFFLED, THEN THEY MUST'VE KILLED HIM...BLAST IT! DAMN SHAME--WELL, YOU BE MORE CAREFUL--AND KEEP ME POSTED ON ANY FURTHER DEVELOPMENTS...

BERLIN    S        MOSCOW

I SHALL...HOPEFULLY, I CAN SLIP AWAY FROM THE PACK SO I CAN TAKE A LOOK AROUND--I'LL BE--

CRASH!
SMASH!

ARGH! RUFFIANS! SPIES! INFILTRATORS! KILL THEM!

WUP! JUST FOUND MY EXIT! OVER AND OUT, CHIEF!...

?

YOU BLOODY HOOLIGAN! WHAT ARE YOU EVEN DOING HERE?!

SAME AS YOU-- TAKING DOWN THESE THUGS!

WHAT? ARE YOU GOING TO BLOW THIS PLACE SKY HIGH NOW? LIKE YOU DID THE PIETER B GALLERY?

PFF--WE DON'T USE GUNS OR BOMBS, WE WERE FRAMED! WE WERE ALL SET TO DEFACE THAT JOINT, BUT THEN-- THAT--THAT--FLAMINGO BIRD TOSSED A BUNDLE OF DYNAMITE AT OUR FEET! SHE KNEW WE'D BE THERE THAT NIGHT...SO, WHEN WE CHUCKED IT AWAY, THAT ONLY MADE US LOOK LIKE THE SABOTEURS TRYING TO BLOW UP THE GALLERY...

FAIR ENOUGH. BUT THAT'S EXACTLY WHY YOU SHOULDN'T BE HERE NOW! YOU'RE OUT OF YOUR DEPTH--GO...MI-6 WILL HANDLE THINGS FROM HERE...

YOU WILL HANDLE THINGS SIDE BY SIDE WITH LEPUS: LIBERATING EUROPEAN PROVINCES UNDER SOVIETISM!

CRIKEY! DID YOU NOT HEAR A WORD I'VE--

'EY!

!

HEY! WHERE'D YOU TWO COME FROM?! GET DOWN FROM HERE!

RUN!

!

BANG! BANG!

BANG!

JEEZ, YOU'D THINK THIS STEEL DOOR WOULDN'T NEED TO BE BARRICADED!

THEY ARE GILA MONSTERS! DON'T WORRY--MI-6 ARE ON THE WAY!

YES, BUT HOW LONG UNTIL THEY GET HERE?

SOON, LET'S HOPE! DAMN, WISH THERE WERE SOME OTHER WAY OUT OF THIS ROOM!

AND I KINDA WISH I HAD A GUN NOW!...

WE GOT 'EM NOW, BROTHER!

YOU CAN'T <u>DO</u> THIS, MAN!

MOVE IT, BUNNY!

WAIT--LET HER GO A MINUTE...

LISTEN, YOU'VE GOT TO COME WITH US...WE NEED TO ASK YOU SOME QUESTIONS...ABOUT THAT BOMBING IN BELGIUM...

BUT--

HEY!

I TOLD THAT SEAL WE DIDN'T BOMB THAT GALLERY!

'EY!

NOT THE PIETER B GALLERY, AN APARTMENT BUILDING--MILES McKELLAR'S HIDEOUT.

WE DIDN'T BOMB THAT PLACE, EITHER! <u>NO</u> ONE DID! AND WE DON'T USE BOMBS.

"NO ONE DID"?...

NO, AND BEFORE--

HEY! YOU! BEFORE YOU CART THAT BIRD OFF TO PRISON, MAKE SURE HE DOESN'T MOLT ON YOU!

!

?

SHHHHH!

"MOLT"?

**YES**, YOU DOLTS! THAT BIRD IS MILES McKELLER!

AND HE'S A PHOENIX!

SHUT UP!

THAT VOICE! IT *IS* McKELLER! OF COURSE--THAT WAS HOW YOU ESCAPED PRISON YEARS AGO!

**RRRRRR!**
DAMN RABBIT FIEND!

YOU DOUBLE-CROSSING SNEAK! THAT'S HOW YOU ALWAYS GET AWAY--ALL THESE YEARS--PRISON, BOMBINGS...HA. WELL, THE NEXT TIME WE FIND A PILE OF DUST IN YOUR PRISON CELL WE WON'T BE SWEEPING IT AWAY, YOU CAN COUNT ON THAT.

IMPERIALIST PIGS! THIS ISN'T OVER!

OKAY, BOYS... TAKE THIS FIREBIRD AWAY AND LET THESE THREE GIRLS GO.

LET'S GO!

YOU HAVEN'T SEEN THE LAST OF MILES McKELLER! NO PRISON CAN EVER HOLD ME!

GREAT WORK YOU TWO--IT WAS A LITTLE ROCKY THERE FOR A WHILE, BUT WE DID IT!

SO WHATTA YA SAY? WANT A LIFT?

YEAH! BEATS GOIN' BACK BY BOAT!

MALCOLM? WHAT IS IT?

I JUST--I WANTED TO FIND THE CORTEN-STEEL PHOENIX...

HA, HA, HA! WHAT DOES THAT MATTER NOW? COME ON, GET IN!

WHUP WHUP WHUP WHUP WHUP WHUP WHUP WHUP WHUP

EHH--ALL RIGHT...

DOESN'T IT BOTHER YOU, THOUGH?